REVERSE
THE DEVIL'S DECISION

MIKE PURKEY

CREATION
HOUSE

REVERSE THE DEVIL'S DECISION by Mike Purkey
Published by Creation House
A part of Strang Communications Company
600 Rinehart Road
Lake Mary, Florida 32746
www.creationhouse.com

Unless otherwise noted, all Scripture quotations are from the New
King James Version of the Bible. Copyright © 1979, 1980, 1982 by
Thomas Nelson, Inc., publishers. Used by permission.

Scripture quotations marked AMP are from the Amplified Bible.
Old Testament copyright © 1965, 1987 by the Zondervan
Corporation. The Amplified New Testament copyright © 1954,
1958, 1987 by the Lockman Foundation. Used by permission.

Scripture quotations marked KJV are from the King James Version
of the Bible.

Scripture quotations marked NAS are from the New American
Standard Bible. Copyright © 1960, 1962, 1963, 1968, 1971, 1972,
1973, 1975, 1977 by the Lockman Foundation. Used by permission. (www.Lockman.org)

Scripture quotations marked NIV are from the Holy Bible, New
International Version. Copyright © 1973, 1978, 1984,
International Bible Society. Used by permission.

Scripture quotations marked THE MESSAGE are from The Message,
copyright © 1993, 1994, 1995. Used by permission of NavPress
Publishing Group.

Library of Congress Catalog Card Number: 00-103903
International Standard Book Number: 0-88419-699-2

0 1 2 3 4 5 6 7 VERSA 8 7 6 5 4 3 2 1
Printed in the United States of America

Dedication

To my wife, Mary, who for more than thirty years has been my faithful companion, ardent supporter, friend and lover. I will be forever grateful to the Lord for joining us as man and wife. Mary, you are constantly helping me to be the person God wants me to be.

To my sons, Matthew and Jonathan. Never could a father be more proud of his sons than I am of you. As we labor together in the full-time work of the Lord, we will, with God's help, *Reverse the Devil's Decision.*

Contents

Introduction

Fastening a Lid on Your Tupperware

Y OU'LL NEVER MAKE *it. Your airplane is going to crash before you ever get to your destination.* Driving alone in my car en route to Kansas City International Airport, I was bombarded with an overwhelming sense of fear that I had never before experienced. In less than an hour my plane would depart, taking me to a city where I was scheduled to speak to a congregation about the victory we as believers have in Christ.

The only problem was, I was losing a personal battle to the panic attack I was experiencing in my car!

Who do you think you are to speak to that congregation? You have nothing to say to those people. What began as a sinking feeling before I left home quickly intensified into an unexplainable fear I could barely control.

My heart began racing at full throttle. My breathing, meanwhile, grew increasingly shorter and more shallow.

Although the temperature in my car was normal, I felt as if I were swimming in a sea of perspiration. *Once I get out of this car, I'll be OK,* I reassured myself. But by the time I pulled into the airport parking lot, I was a mess.

Adding insult to injury, I couldn't find a parking space. The longer I weaved in and out of the lot, the more frustrated I became. Once I finally found a place to park—much farther away from the entrance than I preferred—I unloaded my bags and began lugging them to the terminal.

Your life is doomed. It's over. You have no purpose. Breathing the fresh air did nothing to relieve me of my uncontrollable thoughts. Entering the airport, I was immediately overwhelmed by the avalanche of people who seemed to be crashing in on my ever-decreasing comfort zone. *How could I have thoughts like this?* I asked myself. *I'm a pastor! What's wrong with me?*

No matter how hard I tried, I just couldn't shake myself free from those terrible fears. Although I had flown countless times before, for the first time I just couldn't get myself to board that airplane. Finally, I walked to a nearby phone booth to call the pastor of the church where I was scheduled to speak.

Trembling, I punched in the numbers on the phone. When my dear friend answered, I attempted to vaguely explain. "Pastor, this is Mike Purkey. I'm sorry, but something suddenly came up that prevents me from leaving town. Please accept my sincerest apology, but I just can't make it to your church for the service tonight."

The pastor graciously accepted my apology. I felt guilty about not offering a better explanation, but to be

2

honest, I was just too embarrassed to share with him the real reason why I was canceling.

Oddly enough, driving home from the airport I began feeling much better. I asked myself, *How can I feel so much better now, when I felt so bad just an hour ago?*

Following that traumatic episode, my life returned to normal. In retrospect, I figured it was just a fluke, a one-time occurrence.

On the one hand, I did feel better—especially compared to the panic attack I had experienced. But on the other hand, I also struggled with lingering guilt. How could I be so weak that I would give in to a spirit of fear? I was aggravated and frustrated with myself. Out of embarrassment, I hid my reasons for not going on the trip.

FACING MY FEAR...AGAIN

SEVERAL MONTHS LATER those same feelings of fear and despondency resurfaced. This time it happened while I was at home—not on the way to the airport. They were never problems that raged out of control; they were more like a lingering cloud that followed me wherever I went. More out of denial than faith, I ignored the feelings, hoping they would fade away. But they didn't.

I finally realized that my inactivity would do nothing to solve the problem. If I didn't nip this in the bud, it would come back into my life over and over again. Inwardly I knew that the longer I waited to face it, the harder it would be to overcome. Determined to deal with my problem, I began to pray.

As I began seeking God about my overwhelming feelings of fear, panic and despondency, I realized that the devil had made a decision concerning my life. He didn't want me speaking at that church, so he threw whatever he could find at me to prevent me from going.

The decision of the devil was to torment me, to scare me into acting out of fear. And the tactics he was using on me are no different than the ones he uses on all of us. He tells us:

- "You'll never make it."
- "You'll die early."
- "Your children won't live for God."
- "You're always going to be sick."
- "You're worthless."

I was feeling oppressed when I had no reason to be oppressed. I was afraid when I had nothing to fear. Unfortunately, because I believed the devil's lies, I had given him the upper hand in preventing me from fulfilling the will of God in my life.

I had decided to serve God, but the devil had made a decision of his own. The devil decided to stop me. I realized that in order to fulfill the call of God upon my life, I needed to reverse the devil's decision!

In order to reverse the devil's decision, I had to re-examine what the Word of God has to say about my life, and I had to act upon it. As my faith went into action, I began winning the battle over the devil's decision against me.

The Bible instructs us to fight the good fight of faith (1 Tim. 6:12). My particular skirmish to overcome those fears lasted a couple of weeks. Some people are delivered instantaneously, but most of us must walk out our deliverance through obedience and the Word of God.

My recovery from this experience inspired me to write this book.

FASTEN THE LID ON YOUR TUPPERWARE

EVERY DAY, MILLIONS of blood-bought, Spirit-filled believers accept the devil's decisions regarding their lives. They become satisfied with poverty, sickness, fear and defeat. They live their lives on the run from whatever the enemy happens to be throwing in their direction at the time. You may be one of them.

Dealing with the enemy of our soul is like fastening a lid on a Tupperware bowl. Just as you get one end clamped shut, the other end pops up. If we aren't determined to reverse completely the devil's decisions in our lives, we can get the victory in one area—only to find a similar problem resurfacing somewhere else.

My prayer is that this book will release you into walking the life of victory and anointing that God has prepared for you and every believer to live. I am convinced stories similar to my own are played out in the lives of countless believers—leaders and nonleaders alike. One of Satan's strategies is to fool an individual into believing that he or she is the only one struggling. Satan lives in the shadows, but when we bring our struggles and his deceptive schemes into the light, we find healing, deliverance, victory and freedom.

REVERSE THE DEVIL'S DECISION

A FEW MONTHS after winning the victory over my own struggle, I was on my way to the airport to fly out and speak at another engagement. As I drove, a news bulletin flashed on the radio announcing that a well-known celebrity had just perished in a plane crash. Immediately, those same feelings of fear I had felt a few months earlier began welling up inside me. Although I felt uneasy, I continued driving ahead. This time was different, though. I was able to call the enemy out of the shadows. As I exposed his schemes to the light of God's Word, I quickly broke through his oppression. As a result of my experience, I'm stronger now than I have ever been.

The apostle Paul wrote "We are not ignorant of his [Satan's] schemes" (2 Cor. 2:11, NAS). My goal is not to give the enemy any more press than he already has. But I do want to expose his schemes so that you might not be ignorant of them and accept anything less than God's best.

My prayer for you is that you might see the devil's schemes to hinder your life and that you reverse the devil's decision and find nothing short of God's very best.

May God bless you as you read.

SECTION I
KNOWING YOUR ENEMY

Chapter 1

The Devil Wants You As His Slave

S ATAN IS A deceiver. When it comes to our freedom in Christ, Satan will try to make God's people feel more confused than a termite in a yo-yo. Let me explain what I mean.

When my wife, Mary, and I started out in the ministry, we traveled around the country as evangelists with our two young boys, preaching, singing and touching lives with the gospel of Jesus Christ. As you can imagine, we lived on faith and love for each other in those early years, with very little else.

Just about everything we owned was invested in our black Chevy van. We traveled in it, slept in it, raised our two young boys in it and piled all of our equipment, including our sound equipment, into the back.

Early one cold, rainy winter morning on our way back from preaching at a little church, our two boys were still sound asleep in a small, economy motel room. I pulled the van in front of our room and loaded it up. Leaving the engine on to take the chill out of the van, I went into the room to pick up the sleeping youngsters to carry them out.

I bundled up Matt, my oldest boy, in a blanket and started to walk out to the van when the tires screeched as it pulled away. I ran down the road with Matt in my arms, yelling, "Hey, stop! That's my van! Stop! Stop! Stop!" I chased that thief halfway down the road yelling, but it was useless. Breathless, I stood in the middle of the road in stunned horror as I watched everything we owned speed away. Our ministry was gone. Our home, our transportation, our expensive equipment—all gone. We were devastated in every way, emotionally, financially and in our ministry. The devil had tried to ruin us completely, and he almost did.

We never recovered that van or any of our possessions inside, but I learned a hard lesson about the devil that I've never forgotten.

The devil wants to destroy you and your ministry. He wants to rob you, break you and use the pain and discouragement of that loss to knock you down and control you so that you'll never again be effective for the kingdom of God. The devil has made a decision about your life. He intends to make you his slave so that you'll never be able to serve Jesus Christ. Like a wicked, powerful judge, he has handed down his evil verdict against you to his demonic forces. He has a carefully laid strategy to put you in bondage forever. The devil tried to rob Mary and me and use that loss and discouragement to lock us into a prison of bondage. And he'll try to do the same to you if you let him.

Satan Wants to Rob You!

John 10:10 tells us, "The thief comes only to steal, and kill, and destroy" (NAS). Satan's only interest in you is to steal, kill and destroy what is rightfully yours. He wants to steal everything you and I have as believers: our joy, health, peace, success, family, mind and every good thing God has given to us.

The devil tells us how bad we are, how weak and wicked we are, condemning us for all our faults and short-comings. He tells us, "You might as well give up. There's no use for you to try to live for God. You're a mess! You're a failure! You're guilty!" He tells us, "You're a slave," when God has given us freedom.

Then the devil announces his sentence against us:

- "You are going to have financial problems."
- "You are going to have family trouble."
- "You are going to spend the rest of your life alone and depressed."
- "Your children are going to break your heart and end up in sin."
- "Your loved ones will never be saved."

Just why does the devil want you to accept less than God's best for your life? He's terrified of whom God plans for you to be. Both God and the devil have plans for your life. God says this:

> "For I know the plans I have for you," declares the LORD, "plans to prosper you and not to harm you, plans to give you hope and a future."
>
> —JEREMIAH 29:11, NIV

God plans for us to walk in freedom as bold followers of Christ. But Satan can sometimes get an advantage over us because we didn't start out that way. Before we met Christ, we were the devil's slaves.

WE ARE FREE IN CHRIST

WE'RE ALL BORN as slaves to sin. Jesus said, "Most assuredly, I say to you, whoever commits sin is a slave of sin" (John 8:34). But thanks be to God, when we give our lives to Christ, Jesus transfers us from slavery to sin into a new kind of slavery—slavery to righteousness. "And having been set free from sin, you became slaves of righteousness" (Rom. 6:18). Our compulsion to sin is transformed into a desire to pursue the ways of God.

> *Many believers are slaves to righteousness but still abide by the laws governing slavery to sin. In effect, they are content to honor the decision of Satan's lower court.*

Unfortunately, many believers are slaves to righteousness but still abide by the laws governing slavery to sin. In effect, they are content to honor the decision of Satan's lower court.

THE LOWER COURT

EVERY BELIEVER, EVERY day of his or her life, is put on trial by the enemy of his soul—Satan. The Bible describes his activity this way:

So the great dragon was cast out, that serpent of

old, called the Devil and Satan, who deceives the whole world; he was cast to the earth, and his angels were cast out with him. Then I heard a loud voice saying in heaven, "Now salvation, and strength, and the kingdom of our God, and the power of His Christ have come, for the accuser of our brethren, who accused them before our God day and night, has been cast down."

—REVELATION 12:9–10, EMPHASIS ADDED

Many Christians believe the devil is here on earth, sowing seeds of evil, sickness, disease, poverty and disagreement. But he's not. That's the job of his demons. The passage above tells us he stands before God's tribunal day and night falsely accusing you and me. To accuse means "to speak against" or "to make known." In fact, the Greek word for *devil* means "false accuser." He stands before God and says, "They're not worthy. Did You hear what one of Your followers said?"

> *In the lower court, Satan serves as both the prosecuting attorney and the judge. When the odds are stacked against you like that, without any recourse your fate is sealed.*

The literal description of the word *accuse* in Revelation 12:10 gives the picture of a prosecuting attorney in court of law.[1] In the lower court, Satan serves as both the prosecuting attorney and the judge. When the odds are stacked against you like that, without any recourse your fate is sealed.

On our own, we are no match for the deviousness and corruption of the lower court. But praise God, I'm happy to report to you that it doesn't have to be that way. There is a higher court of appeals than the devil. His decision does not have to be final. God will reverse that decision in your life. But first you must appeal the lower court ruling to the higher court of God.

OUR INDEPENDENCE DAY

JESUS PAID FOR us with His blood to free us from the bondages and effects of our sin: fear, hopelessness, sinful habits and so on. Unfortunately, too many Christians hear the decision of Satan's lower court, slump their shoulders and resign in despair. They neglect to appeal to God's Supreme Court of justice. We can reverse the devil's decision for our lives!

You were freed from your slavery to the devil through the cross of Jesus Christ. Can you imagine the futility of returning to a life of slavery after you've already been freed? Some slaves did exactly that following the Civil War. Even more tragic, many more Christians do the same thing. By accepting the decision of the devil—the lower court—those who are free in Christ submit their lives to bondage. The Bible warns us not to let this happen. Galatians 5:1 says, "It was for freedom that Christ set us free; therefore keep standing firm and do not be subject again to a yoke of slavery" (NAS).

GOD'S HIGHER COURT DECISION

OFTENTIMES GOD BLESSES us in spite of our ceaseless wanderings and unbelief. When we choose to believe and act upon God's Word—rejecting the lower court ruling—our faith activates God's plans and hopes for our lives and starts them into motion.

The courts in most countries are built on precedent. In other words, previous court decisions become the standard for later decisions. Once a crime has been committed and a certain course of legal action has been taken, then all other cases have a tendency to be settled in the same manner. Legal precedent saves time and ensures all similar cases are handled the same way.

The Bible is filled with spiritual precedents giving us a record of how God has handled decisions that Satan has made against the children of God.

Job

Satan decided he would take Job's children, his wealth, his health and then cause family and friends to falsely accuse him. The devil wanted to destroy Job; his lower court decision was, "I'll make Job curse God, give up, turn aside and refuse to follow Him."

But Job appealed to the higher court. Job cried out to God, "Though He slay me, yet will I trust Him" (Job 13:15). No matter what happened to him, Job refused to curse God. In the end God gave Job twice as much as he had previously. (See Job 42:10.) Job reversed the devil's decision.

Joseph

The promise of God's wonderful plan was even greater for Joseph. God revealed His plans to Joseph in a wonderful dream. Joseph would become a great ruler. Recognizing that Joseph would play a powerful role in saving the lives of his family—who were God's promised people—Satan decided to stop him. Joseph's dreams must never come true. Satan had Joseph sold into slavery and thrown into jail on false charges, but Joseph never gave up. He appealed to the higher court of heaven. In the end he rose to power in Egypt, second only to Pharoah in influence. And when drought struck his estranged family in Canaan, Joseph was able to provide for them and preserve God's promise. (See Genesis 37–47.)

David

David's promise from God was that he would be king of Israel. Therefore, Satan decided that David must die, and he sent a lion to attack him. But David reversed the devil's decision, and armed with faith in God, he killed the lion. Later Satan sent a bear, but David killed it, too. Then David had a face-to-face showdown with Satan's champion, Goliath, who stood over nine feet tall. When questioned by King Saul as to whether he could destroy Goliath, David appealed to the higher court. David said, "The LORD, who delivered me from the paw of the lion and from the paw of the bear . . . will deliver me from the hand of this Philistine" (1 Sam. 17:37). So Saul permitted David to fight Goliath, and David was victorious. David's act of courage in the face of uncertainty and danger made him a hero in Israel and paved the way for him to succeed Saul as king.

Daniel

Daniel was a man of integrity and prayer who also served in a position of authority and influence for King Darius in what was once Babylon. As Daniel's influence in Persia grew, the devil decided to stop him by killing him. Satan decided, "You will die in the lions' den." The king was tricked into making an edict outlawing prayer to anyone but himself upon penalty of death. But Daniel appealed to a higher court. He refused to stop praying to the one true God, and consequently he was thrown into the lions' den. However, because Daniel refused to abide by the devil's lower court decision, God preserved his life and shut the mouths of the lions. As a result, Daniel's influence was actually increased in the kingdom of Persia. (See Daniel 6.)

The apostle Paul

The apostle Paul was single-handedly turning the world upside down for the gospel. Lives were being changed, people were being won for Christ, churches were being planted and the kingdom of God was expanding throughout the Roman Empire as a result of his work. God had decided that the apostle Paul should bring the message of God's saving power to the Gentiles. But Satan made a decision, too. Satan decided to stop him by killing him before his work was completed. In 2 Corinthians 11, Paul lists various attempts Satan made to enforce his decision:

- Whipped thirty-nine times on five different occasions
- Beaten with rods three times
- Stoned and left for dead once
- Shipwrecked three times, including an entire night and day at sea
- Suffered weariness, pain, hunger, thirst, cold and nakedness

Despite the hardships he endured, Paul kept appealing

to a higher court and reversed the devil's decision. Years later Paul could declare:

> I have fought the good fight, I have finished the course, I have kept the faith; in the future there is laid up for me the crown of righteousness, which the Lord, the righteous Judge, will award to me on that day; and not only to me, but also to all who have loved His appearing.
>
> —2 TIMOTHY 4:7–8, NAS

Jesus

Throughout His ministry, Jesus' life was in danger. Satan's decision was to oppose Him, stop Him and destroy Him and His ministry. Satan decided Jesus should be arrested (John 10:39), stoned (John 8:59) and thrown off a cliff (Luke 4:29–30), yet none of these happened until Jesus fulfilled His purpose here on earth. When Satan finally succeeded in taking Jesus' life, he unknowingly assisted in God's plan to bring salvation to the entire world.

GOD'S PLAN FOR *YOUR* LIFE

NOT ONLY DID Jesus bring us salvation, but He also left us His Holy Spirit so we have His power to overcome Satan and his wicked decisions to hinder us, rob us and destroy us. If you have given your life to Jesus Christ, you now have God and the power of heaven living inside of You. There is no reason in the world why you have to settle for Satan's lower court ruling in your life.

Satan may have made a decision concerning your life, but when you appeal to the higher court, God's decree beats the devil's decision every time! You may have seen freedom from a distance, but have been held in captivity, falsely imprisoned and beaten.

> *Satan may have made a decision concerning your life, but when you appeal to the higher court, God's decree beats the devil's decision every time!*

Jesus said, "Therefore if the Son makes you free, you shall be free indeed" (John 8:36). If Jesus set you free, which He did at the cross, you have no business returning to a pitiful life of slavery that can be avoided altogether. The victory for the devil is not when something terrible has been committed against you—you can expect that from the accuser. The greatest victory for the devil is when you become content with the devil's decision!

The devil tried to knock Mary and me out of ministry, and it wasn't the first time. If we had accepted his decision, our lives wouldn't be where they are today. Don't ever accept Satan's lower court decisions for your life.

You can keep this from ever happening to you by better understanding how the devil tries to fool believers into becoming content with his lower court decisions.

Chapter 2

You Look Like You Could Eat Oats Out of a Two-Inch Pipe

S ATAN IS A thief. He wants to rob you of your joy, beat you, wound you and leave you for dead. The devil wants you so discouraged that your long face will look like you could eat oats out of a two-inch pipe! But in Jesus Christ, no matter what the devil throws at you, you can still win. Let me explain.

To reverse the devil's decision for your life, you must identify what his decision is. Most people don't realize that the devil's work affects us on the same levels as Jesus'—the spiritual, the physical and the emotional— except with completely different goals.

Because it is one of the most studied parables in the Gospels, the story of the Good Samaritan is difficult to read with new eyes. However, once we move past the primary meaning—the importance of loving our neighbor— we begin to see at a deeper level not only the work of

Jesus, but also the work of the devil. As we examine this parable, join me in reading the story of the Good Samaritan with new eyes, and put yourself in the shoes—or make that sandals—of that lonely man walking down the road to Jericho:

> A certain man went down from Jerusalem to Jericho, and fell among thieves, who stripped him of his clothing, wounded him, and departed, leaving him half dead.
>
> Now by chance a certain priest came down that road. And when he saw him, he passed by on the other side. Likewise a Levite, when he arrived at the place, came and looked, and passed by on the other side. But a certain Samaritan, as he journeyed, came where he was. And when he saw him, he had compassion. So he went to him and bandaged his wounds, pouring on oil and wine; and he set him on his own animal, brought him to an inn, and took care of him. On the next day, when he departed, he took out two denarii, gave them to the innkeeper, and said to him, "Take care of him; and whatever more you spend, when I come again, I will repay you."
>
> —Luke 10:30–35

STAY IN JERUSALEM!

AN EASILY OVERLOOKED point in this story—one I rarely hear discussed—is the mistake the central character made right at the outset: He left Jerusalem to go down to Jericho. Because Jerusalem is situated on a hill and Jericho is located down in the Jordan Valley, the man would have to walk down some pretty rugged terrain on a narrow, winding road, ideal for bandits and people evading the law. To discourage attacks from robbers, everyone generally understood the importance of traveling in groups. To make this twenty-mile trek alone was to invite trouble.

Now this man would have avoided the mess entirely had he stayed in Jerusalem. Jerusalem in this parable represents power and anointing. It represents the manifest presence of God. Jericho, on the other hand, was not only lower in elevation, but it was also located on the edge of the Promised Land. Jericho was the farthest you could go from the anointing and still remain in the land of promise.

I know people who, if they had stayed where the power and the anointing were and where the Word of God was going out, would not be in the mess they're in. Instead, they began placing a higher value on convenience than the anointing of the Holy Spirit. I know people who are looking for a church that is closer to home, regardless of whether or not the gospel is being preached there.

> Well, you have to understand, Pastor, we *did* leave Jerusalem to go to Jericho Fellowship. There's nobody getting saved or helped there, but they start at 11 A.M. and they're out by noon so we can beat everybody to the restaurants. It's a little cold, it's dead, it's dry, but at least the pastor keeps his word and we start at 11 A.M., sing two songs, hear three points and a poem and we get out on time.

> Yes, we took our young people out of Jerusalem to go to Jericho. Out where our young people are going, there is no one getting saved or delivered. They run about sixteen to eighteen kids, but it's so nice. They have a nice volleyball net and nice

games. There's not much preaching going on, but it's a wonderful place where everybody is happy and our kids are happy. Well, maybe our kids aren't *that* happy, but they'll adjust. And it was such a chore to get to your church. It was all we could do to get into our Lexus and drive those five miles to attend.

When we depart from what we know is the anointing and the will of God, we make ourselves vulnerable or open to attack. Usually when we walk away from the anointing, we do it alone, so when we get beaten up by the forces of darkness, no one is around to pick us up.

> *When we depart from what we know is the anointing and the will of God, we make ourselves vulnerable or open to attack.*

What's most important is not whether you attend a black church, a white church, a rich church, a respected church or a big church. What's most important is whether it's a "Jesus" church. Is Jesus alive where you are getting fed? You need to do whatever it takes to be where the Holy Ghost is flowing, where people are getting saved, healed and set free from sin. If you have to sell pop bottles in order to buy enough gas to drive across town to get there, then do it.

Whatever you do, stay plugged in where Jesus is real and alive. You see, thieves stay away from Jerusalem. The devil doesn't want to hang around where Jesus is being lifted up and the power of the gospel is presented in the anointing of the Holy Ghost. Somebody at the church may have offended you, you may have to drive across town and the service may run long so you have to stand in line at the restaurant, but stay in Jerusalem.

THE DEVIL'S THREEFOLD MINISTRY

THE MAN IN the parable walked away from God's anointing, and because he was alone, a group of thieves assaulted him. Just as Jerusalem represents the anointing of God and Jericho represents a departure from God's presence, the thieves represent the devil and his demons. In the last chapter, I mentioned that the devil's only interest in you is to steal, kill and destroy what is rightfully yours. He's no better than a two-bit thief.

As we read how the man was assaulted along the road, we begin to see the nature of the devil's threefold strategy in every person's life—especially the believer's.

THE DEVIL DESIRES TO STRIP US

LET'S LOOK AGAIN at the beginning of the story.

> A certain man went down from Jerusalem to Jericho, and fell among thieves, who stripped him of his clothing, wounded him, and departed, leaving him half dead.
>
> —LUKE 10:30

In those times clothing was expensive, and most people owned only a few changes of apparel. It was a valuable commodity. Stripping a man of his clothing robbed him of his dignity and humiliated him before all the people passing by. But above all, it exposed his vulnerability.

The devil comes along and says, "I'd like to get to you,

but you just keep praising the Lord. Every time I send a demon of depression, you start clapping and praising God and dancing in the Holy Spirit." He walks away saying to himself, "I can't get to him because he has the garment of praise on. I need to strip him because I'd like to destroy him."

The devil wants to strip you of your garment of praise. Whatever you do, don't give him your garment of praise. Keep it alive. The devil does whatever he can to hinder God's people from worshiping in spirit and truth, because that draws him into a battle he knows he cannot win. If he can't keep you from coming to church, then he wants you to be as quiet as a church mouse when you come. He doesn't want you to raise your hands and say, "Thank You, Jesus." He doesn't want you to enter the holy of holies where God can really minister to you and change you. He doesn't want you singing praises to God while you drive to work in the morning. No matter how dark the situation you face, never stop using all of your might to praise God.

> *The devil does whatever he can to hinder God's people from worshiping in spirit and truth, because that draws him into a battle he knows he cannot win.*

I find it interesting how some people like to criticize and make fun of churches that are full of life. But then the same folks go to a football game and go crazy. If the world can get crazy about a pigskin that flies back and forth between two poles, then there's no way I'm going to let them stop me from praising the God who doesn't play games. He plays in real-life situations, and He plays for keeps.

The devil wants to strip you of every good thing God wants to work in your life. He wants to strip you of your joy and your excitement in the Lord. He wants you offended and upset. He wants you sitting in a corner mumbling to yourself, defeated, upset, sour-faced and mad at the world. You can always spot the Christians who have already been stripped of their garment of praise because they are negative, grumpy and unhappy.

THE DEVIL DESIRES TO WOUND US

NOTICE, THE THIEVES didn't inflict personal injury on the man until they first stripped him. Once the devil has stripped us of our garment of praise, he knows we can't defend ourselves against his attacks.

We can't always prevent painful experiences from happening, but we can keep the pain from continuing. When we begin dwelling on our pain, we give the devil an opportunity to wound us. Overwhelming disappointment, an agonizing divorce, an upsetting childhood incident or something someone said is all the devil needs to create a wound.

> *We can't always prevent painful experiences from happening, but we can keep the pain from continuing. When we begin dwelling on our pain, we give the devil an opportunity to wound us.*

Once we take the pain personally, we invite the forces of evil to work us over. When we are hurt, we can easily direct our pain toward others, ourselves or both. If we direct our pain toward others, we become mean and easily offended. If we direct our pain toward ourselves, we lose our self-confidence and blame ourselves for any and every problem. Either way we lose our joy and become even more deeply wounded in the process.

People who are wounded become so focused on their pain that they can't see the devil plundering them. Their negative attitude affects them at work, at home and at church. Supervisors don't promote them, family members avoid them and friends abandon them. The joy of the abundant life Jesus promised is virtually nonexistent. People who are deeply wounded can only focus on one thing: their pain.

Many people also direct their pain toward God. They begin to question, "God, how could You just stand there and do nothing while I was suffering? Why didn't You do anything? I thought You were love, but now I know You just don't care." If the pain isn't dealt with, they become embittered against God.

Dealing with the devil's wounds

The best way to deal with the painful wounds the devil inflicts is to acknowledge the pain and give it to God. When we direct our pain toward God, we use it as a weapon. When we give our pain to God, we present it to Him for healing. It's OK to come before Him and say, "I'm bleeding, I'm hurting and I'm half dead." It's OK to go to your pastor and say, "Pastor, I need somebody to lay hands on me, rebuke the enemy and stand on the Word of God with me. I need help, and I need it right now." When we read through the Psalms, we quickly see that the writers didn't hold back from expressing their deepest hurts to God.

Too many of us conclude that acknowledging our pain is walking in unbelief. But the pain has to be directed somewhere. If we don't give it to God, we'll either direct it toward God and drive His presence away from our lives, we'll direct it toward others and drive everyone else away, or we'll direct it toward ourselves and sink into depression and other self-destructive behaviors. God can't heal us until we acknowledge to Him that our pain even exists!

Sometimes our fear of saying the wrong thing prevents us from being real with God. We're afraid that if we trip up and say something negative to God, He'll remove His blessing or we'll lose our healing. Our words are important, but we should never lose sight of the fact that He sees past our words and into our hearts.

THE DEVIL LEAVES US HALF DEAD

AFTER THE DEVIL wounds us, he leaves us half dead. The devil strips us, wounds us and leaves us to die.

But the devil is not nearly as smart as some people think. You see, the devil makes a big mistake by leaving us half dead. If we're half dead, then we're also still half alive! And if we're half alive, there's enough left in us to get back up again, get back in the Word again and get plugged in again into the name of Jesus.

No matter how the devil has knocked you down, it's never too late to get up again. You may feel half dead, but I want to tell you, you're also half alive! You may have been abiding by the decision of the lower court, but you can appeal to the Supreme Court of Justice!

The reason you can get up is because Jesus has a fourfold ministry that by far surpasses anything the devil can do to you.

JESUS' FOURFOLD MINISTRY

THE MAN IN our story was beaten and left at the side of the road for dead, but he refused to die. People more concerned with playing church than being the church walked right past him, but they didn't want to dirty their hands by messing with him.

> Now by chance a certain priest came down that road. And when he saw him, he passed by on the other side. Likewise a Levite, when he arrived at the place, came and looked, and passed by on the other side.
>
> —LUKE 10:31–32

But then the Good Samaritan passed by:

> But a certain Samaritan, as he journeyed, came where he was. And when he saw him, he had compassion. So he went to him and bandaged his wounds, pouring on oil and wine; and he set him on his own animal, brought him to an inn, and took care of him. On the next day, when he departed, he took out two denarii, gave them to the innkeeper, and said to him, "Take care of him; and whatever more you spend, when I come again, I will repay you."
>
> —LUKE 10:33–35

When we realize Jesus is our Good Samaritan, we begin to see His fourfold ministry.

First, He meets us where we are.

When the Good Samaritan saw the man lying on the road, nearly dead, He did what no one else would do.

He got involved in the man's deliverance.

Aren't you glad that when we're unable or unwilling to go to Him, Jesus, the Good Samaritan, still comes to us? When we're ashamed of our sin, Jesus comes beside us and accepts us. Romans 5:8 tells us, "But God demonstrates His own love toward us, in that while we were still sinners, Christ died for us."

I am so glad that when I can't reach Him, He still reaches out to me at just the right time. Jesus is the kind of Savior that, when we're overcome by sin and shame that causes us to push Him away and say we don't want anything else to do with Him, will still deal with us and work with us.

Jesus doesn't say, "I'll wait until you get your act together before I'll help you." He doesn't hold to the common misconception that "God helps those who help themselves." That battered and beaten man on the road could do nothing to help himself.

> *Even when we're responsible for the terrible spiritual condition in which we find ourselves, Jesus still sees us through His eyes of compassion and meets us where we are.*

By touching a man who was possibly dead, the Good Samaritan risked becoming defiled. But his compassion for a man he didn't know exceeded his concern about being defiled. In fact, the passage describes the Good Samaritan's first reaction when he came upon the beaten man: "And when he saw him, he had compassion" (Luke 10:33). Even when we're responsible for the terrible spiritual condition in which we find ourselves, Jesus still sees us through His eyes of compassion and meets us where we are.

The devil deserts us, but Jesus meets us where we are.

Second, He binds up our wounds.

When the Good Samaritan found the man lying on the side of the road, he did what no one else would do. He walked over and began to care for him. He poured some oil and wine over the wounds in order to clean and disinfect them, then bandaged the wounds in order to stop the bleeding and to start the man's recovery.

Jesus isn't interested in watching us suffer any longer than we have to. He came to bring healing and wholeness into our lives—to build us up, not tear us down. Jesus pours the oil of the Holy Spirit over our wounds to soothe us. Then He pours the wine of His blood into our wounds in order to bring forgiveness and healing. Last of all, He covers our wounds to prevent infection from worsening our condition.

The devil strips us, but Jesus binds up our wounds.

Third, He picks us up and carries us.

The Good Samaritan picked up the injured man and set him on his own beast. The fellow was wounded and hurt, but he was still riding.

When we can't go any further, when we can't even get up off the ground, Jesus picks us up and carries us. The man may have been unconscious and unable to get up by himself, but it didn't matter, because the Good Samaritan was there. Sometimes we're in so much pain we don't even realize Jesus is carrying us until after we've recovered.

The devil has decided that we should be beaten and thrown into a ditch, but Jesus overrules the devil's decision by picking us up and carrying us.

The devil beats us down, but Jesus lifts us up and carries us.

Fourth, Jesus stays by our side until we're out of danger.

The Good Samaritan brought the injured man to an inn where he took care of him. Luke 10 tells us that the Good Samaritan not only paid the injured man's expenses and motel room, but he stayed by his side until the next day.

He bandaged him and poured oil and wine into his hurts and cuts. Why would he want to stay up all night and take care of him? The Good Samaritan understood something that medical science knows today. The first twenty-four hours after an injury or an operation are critical. In order for a patient's recovery to be monitored, he is usually placed in the Intensive Care Unit (ICU). If he can make it through those first twenty-four hours, there's a good chance he'll recover.

You may feel as if you're living in ICU. You've been robbed, hurt, wounded and abandoned. But thank God, Jesus came down to sit up all night with you. Jesus will be there at the foot of your bed taking care of you. Why is that important? Because the devil is ruthless. He's still cruising around your house. He's still shaking your locks. He's still trying to find a way to get in and mess you up and take you out. He's not satisfied that you're bruised a little bit. He wants to totally destroy you.

> *You may feel as if you're living in ICU. You've been robbed, hurt, wounded and abandoned. But thank God, Jesus came down to sit up all night with you. Jesus will be there at the foot of your bed taking care of you.*

But we have Someone sitting at the foot of our beds telling us, "I'll stay here as long as I have to stay. The devil can rattle your locks and shake your door as much as he wants, but that's all right. I'll protect you and stay by your side until you're out of danger."

When the devil leaves us half dead, Jesus stays with us until we're out of danger.

JESUS CAME DOWN SO WE COULD GET UP!

JESUS IS NOT afraid to go where you are, into the mess that you're in and pull you out. Two thousand years ago, Jesus came down so those who are down could get up. Those who are down in alcohol, perversion, drugs, fear, depression, defeat and anything else the devil might throw at them can rise up from their ditch in Jesus' name. Jesus came down and reversed the devil's decision so you could get up.

No matter how down you may be, no matter how far you may stray, no matter how wounded you may feel, no matter how deep in sin or bound up in habits you may have become, Jesus can meet you where you are. He will bind your wounds, pick you up, carry you to safety and stay by your side until you're out of danger. You don't have to live with the devil's decision for your life–Jesus is with you!

Chapter 3

Take a Lickin', but Keep On Tickin'

SATAN IS A liar. When you decide to follow God's plan and walk in His best for your life, conflict will follow. He will lie to you and lie to others about you. He'll turn others against you to try to get you to give up on God's best. But you can take a lickin' and keep on tickin'! Let me explain.

Two lies about living the life of faith fill the thinking of many Christians. We all will tend to gravitate toward one or the other.

The first one goes like this: If you do nice things, than nice things will always happen to you. Some people in the church have promoted the idea that if you really trust God, you shouldn't have to suffer. Bad things only happen to bad people. If something bad happens to you, then you must be a bad person or you must have done something that was really bad. This is not only false, but it's also heresy. Jesus was the only sinless man, yet He suffered on a cross without any good, justifiable reason. The Bible says, "Many are the afflictions of the righteous, but the LORD delivers him out of them all" (Ps. 34:19).

The second lie robs you of your faith. It says, "There is nothing you can do to change the problems in your life." Others in the church teach that you must learn to live with your sickness, disease, poverty or any other mess in your life. Your only hope is in the hereafter. Yet Jesus told His disciples, "Most assuredly, I say to you, he who believes in Me, the works that I do he will do also; and greater works than these he will do, because I go to My Father" (John 14:12). To a great extent, Jesus' ministry involved delivering the oppressed and healing the sick. The Holy Spirit power He gave His followers at Pentecost is the same power He gives to you today to rise above your problems in this life and live a life of victory. You can put your foot where it belongs—on the devil's neck—and choke him. You can crush the serpent's head and let him know that it's time you begin to reign in life and not let him reign over you.

You can name it, claim it, read everybody's book and listen to everybody's tape on five steps to a blessing and ten steps on how to get out of your mess. The truth of it is, you're going to have to understand that when you get outside of the church building, you're going to have to walk the walk, talk the talk and learn to stand up in faith in the name of Jesus. And the time to build your faith is not when you are in a storm; it's before the storm ever comes. We're having to rethink our philosophies; we've done everything everybody said to do, but storms are continuing to rage in our lives. God has promised to be with us during the storm. He'll take us through and be our helper. The simplicity of the truth lies in the concept that they that live godly lives in Christ Jesus shall suffer persecution.

In this chapter I want to blast both theories to pieces so you can rise up as a champion full of faith, power and authority in Jesus' name.

Bad things *do* happen to good people, but you can overcome them. You can live in constant victory no matter what decision the devil has made concerning your life. You have the name of Jesus, the blood of Jesus and the Word of God. These are the weapons that will give you the authority and ability to take your foot and put it where it belongs: right on the serpent's head. The devil is not supposed to rule you, control you, manipulate you or make your life miserable. You can put him under your feet. That's where he belongs.

> *You can live in constant victory no matter what decision the devil has made concerning your life.*

THE COST OF SWITCHING SIDES

LET'S LOOK AT a group of people who decided to follow after righteousness and got into trouble as a result, but then they overcame by the power of God:

> Therefore Adoni-Zedek king of Jerusalem sent to Hoham king of Hebron, Piram king of Jarmuth, Japhia king of Lachish, and Debir king of Eglon, saying, "Come up to me and help me, that we

may attack Gibeon, for it has made peace with
Joshua and with the children of Israel."

—JOSHUA 10:3–4

The children of Israel had just entered the Promised
Land. Along the way, word spread among the surrounding nations that Israel carried a military advantage
none of her enemies could counter: They had the
power of the one true God. The Gibeonites watched as
God helped the children of Israel defeat the inhabitants
of Jericho and Ai. As they saw God's power at work,
they knew they were outmatched. So rather than fight
the power of God, they decided to join the Israelites.

That's what will happen to you. When people see
that God is on your side, anyone who wants to win will
want to join you. No one wants to be on the losing side.
That's why churches need to learn how to walk in the
anointing of the Holy Ghost and the signs that follow.
When God is moving in your ministry—really moving—
you won't be able to keep the people away.

Through deceptive means the Gibeonites convinced
Israel to agree to a peace treaty. In exchange for their
safety, the Gibeonites pledged to serve as woodcutters
and water carriers.

Switching allegiances from darkness to light might
prevent a run-in with God, but that doesn't mean you
won't make someone mad. The surrounding nations—
friends of the Gibeonites—didn't like the idea that one
of their own was jumping sides.

People will like you as long as you run in their crowd.
But if you quit running with them, they won't like you
anymore. The moment you decide you want to get into

the Word, start living right and serving Jesus, then everybody gets mad—their claws grow out, and they get mean and angry!

This was the mess the Gibeonites faced in Joshua 10. Up to that point they had been heathens and idolaters working for the wrong side. But when they heard about the power of God at Jericho and Ai, when they saw how God worked for His people, how God moved mightily and powerfully, they said, "We don't know about everybody else, but we're going to change sides. We're going to get on the side of the *El Shaddai* God who is more than enough. We're going to get on the side of Abraham, Isaac and Jacob."

You need to understand how important it is that you get in with the right God. You must plug in to the one true God. I'm not talking about Muhammad. I'm not talking about Buddha. I'm not talking about a social gospel. I'm talking about the God of the universe who holds the world in the palm of His hand. I'm talking about a God who sent Jesus Christ into this world two thousand years ago. You'd better get on the right side, because if God is for you, then no one can stand against you—not the devil, not the world. If God is on your side, you can move forward. If all you have left is God, you have enough to start over again and be victorious.

People love you until you leave them. The moment you decide to follow God's calling on your life, to pursue the ways of God, the devil puts you on his hit list. People who couldn't even get along before will start getting along for a season if they think they can take you down. People start getting attitudes about you. They start talking behind your back. They get on the phone and ask each other, "What's wrong with Mike? He just isn't fun anymore. He doesn't tell the dirty jokes he used to. Instead he talks about Jesus. He spends time with his family, and he's always going to church. I hear he's got religion."

When people get an attitude about you, just look them right in the eye and tell them nicely, "I can take a licking but keep on ticking in the name of Jesus!"

> *When people get an attitude about you, just look them right in the eye and tell them nicely, "I can take a licking but keep on ticking in the name of Jesus!"*

First Peter 5:8 tells us, "Be sober, be vigilant; because your adversary the devil walks about like a roaring lion, seeking whom he may devour." If the devil is seeking people "whom he may devour," that means there are some people whom he can't devour.

The devil can't come stomping in on your life any time and any way he wants. If you belong to Jesus, you're covered by the blood of the Lamb. You have protection by the blood of Jesus. You have power in the word of your testimony and in your knowledge of the Word of God in your life. That's what gets the devil so frustrated and mad. You go through trials and tribulations. You suffer sickness in your body. You deal with all kinds of obstacles, but hell is frustrated with you because you stay in the Word and keep going to church.

You take everything the devil throws at you, but you don't act any different. You just keep clapping your hands and singing and shouting and dancing and praising God. The doctor tells you that you are going to die, but you just keep coming to church. The lawyer tells you that you're going broke, but you tell your lawyer, "My God shall supply all [my] need[s] according to His riches in glory by Christ Jesus" (Phil. 4:19).

Hell doesn't understand why you keep smiling. The devil doesn't understand why you keep talking life while everybody else is talking death. Hell doesn't understand how you can keep coming to church when everybody else in the neighborhood is out on their boat or watching television. "I know whom I have believed and am persuaded that He is able to keep what I have committed to Him until that Day" (1 Tim. 1:12).

> Therefore the five kings of the Amorites, the king of Jerusalem, the king of Hebron, the king of Jarmuth, the king of Lachish, and the king of Eglon, gathered together and went up, they and all their armies, and camped before Gibeon and made war against it.
>
> —JOSHUA 10:5

The five major kings in the region—former allies of Gibeon—formed a confederation to attack the Gibeonites. People who couldn't even get along before started getting along for a season in order to take the Gibeonites down. Then they mobilized their armies and camped outside the city of Gibeon.

EVEN THE LONE RANGER HAD TONTO

AT THIS POINT the Gibeonites faced two choices. First, they could switch allegiances back to their former allies. With the armies of the confederation camped outside

Gibeon, the threats were difficult to ignore: "We'll destroy you unless you come back." "Israel doesn't care about you; they'll kill you when they're finished using you." "If you abandon us, you won't have anyone left."

The devil is always mouthing off. He lies to us and threatens us to keep us from allying ourselves with God. He says, "If you sell out to Jesus, your friends will desert you; they'll turn on you, and no one will like you." And part of what he says *is* true. When we give ourselves completely to God we find that the things we used to do with our old cronies just aren't fun anymore. We may lose some friendships along the way, but that doesn't mean we're abandoned.

> *Even the Lone Ranger had Tonto.*

Their second choice was to seek help from not only the God of Israel, but also the Israel of God. The Gibeonites had the sense to do what a lot of us do not do: They called for backup. That's why we need the church. We all need somebody to lean on. Even the Lone Ranger had Tonto.

People pray, "Jesus, I need Your help," but then neglect to go to the body of Christ for support. You need the church to stand with you and hold you up when you're facing the devil's decisions for your life. When the world turns on you, turn to Jesus and His people. The reaction of those who turned against the Gibeonites should have come as no surprise.

GET READY TO FIGHT

THE APOSTLE PAUL wrote, "Therefore put on the full armor of God, so that *when the day of evil comes*, you may be able to stand your ground, and after you have done everything, to stand" (Eph. 6:13, NIV, emphasis added). The day you choose to align yourself with righteousness, godliness and the armies of God is the day you enter a battle that you cannot avoid. The Bible doesn't say that the day of evil *might* come. It says that the day of evil *will* come. It may be sooner, it may be later, but it *will* come.

The confederation of kings understood that when Gibeon switched sides, it strengthened Israel's position and weakened theirs. In the same way, Satan understands that when we become an active soldier in the army of God, we pose an imminent threat because we weaken his position and strengthen God's. It is for this reason that he makes a decision against us. He decides to do whatever he can to neutralize us.

It doesn't matter how many faith seminars you attend, how much you read your Bible or how much you pray. These things won't help you avoid the battle. But they *will* prepare you for the battles you will inevitably face. Jesus never promised that we would avoid the storm, but He did promise to walk with us right through the middle of the storm until we are safe on the other side. He'll take us through and be our helper.

The fact is, the Bible tells us that "all who desire to live godly in Christ Jesus will suffer persecution" (2 Tim. 3:12).

> *Jesus never promised that we would avoid the storm, but He did promise to walk with us right through the middle of the storm until we are safe on the other side.*

Living a godly life, in fact, means you will actually attract attacks. Drive through any major city and you will find high-crime areas with twelve- and thirteen-year-old children carrying guns and knives. You may even witness a drive-by shooting or a drug deal gone bad. Strangely enough, in the same drug-infested neighborhoods you will also see people clothed in rags pushing old grocery carts filled with other people's leftovers. Have you ever wondered why nobody is robbing them or knifing them or shooting them? They're part of the system. These individuals pose no threat to the balance of power in that community. They have nothing in their possession that anybody wants. If your enemy the devil comes against you, it's only because you have something to offer.

Are you under attack because of your stand for God? Don't get discouraged. Let me share some important keys that will cause you to conquer your enemies when it feels as if every demon in hell is coming against you.

Chapter 4

When All Hail Breaks Loose

W HEN THE GIBEONITES switched allegiances to the God of Israel, they stirred up a hornet's nest among their former allies. Don't be shocked when all hail breaks loose against you—because it will.

If you're on the devil's hit list—it's because of where you're headed. The enemy is not fighting you over where you are; he's fighting you over where you're going. The devil is terrified about where you are headed. He's terrified about the anointing on your life. He's terrified about your stand and your walk with Christ and the power of the Holy Ghost that's on you. The devil's decision is to abort God's purpose, God's mission and God's plan in your life. He hasn't changed much; he tried to do the same to the Gibeonites. Let's take a look.

> *The enemy is not fighting you over where you are; he's fighting you over where you're going. The devil is is terrified about where you are headed.*

When the Gibeonites switched allegiances from God's enemies, they stirred up a hornet's nest among their former allies. Don't be shocked when the same thing happens to you. The Gibeonites also called upon God's people by sending a desperate cry to Joshua, "We need you to back us up."

The devil decided that the Gibeonites should die before joining forces with the armies of God. Had Gibeon done nothing, they would have all been slaughtered. But they called on Joshua to bring deliverance to their people.

Joshua's response in bringing deliverance to the Gibeonites gives us three important keys in reversing the devil's decision for our lives.

CONFRONT THE ENEMY

YOU MUST CONFRONT the enemy because running is not an option. You'll never get the victory by avoiding your problems. Even if you can get away from your circumstances, Satan will fight you on the inside through thoughts and feelings that flood your mind and heart. And you cannot run from your own mind. Your greatest fight takes place between your ears.

Don't allow your past to destroy your future. Learn to confront your enemies, no matter what they are.

There is no such thing as a victory without a confrontation. You might be thinking, "Oh, I could never do that. I just like to tiptoe through the tulips, sing the Word and just float from glory to glory." Well, you'd better confront some things, or you'll always be running away from your problems.

> *There is no such thing as a victory without a confrontation.*

A church that refuses to confront its problems can end up becoming a three-ring circus, and when the show is over, the people exit and leave you to clean up the mess.

Parents who avoid confronting their children and their children's problems wind up with families full of misery and strife. But when you confront your children in their sin, you also confront the one who stands *behind* their sin. When you confront an individual in his or her sin, you resist the enemy who is darkening that person's heart and mind. The Bible says that when you resist the devil, he has to flee. By confronting sin instead of burying your head in the sand, you turn the light on in that dark place and open a door of deliverance to everyone involved.

When I use the word *confront*, I don't mean that you should be vicious or mean-spirited. I mean you should speak the truth in love to the person or problem, standing up for what the Word of God says, knowing your spiritual rights and letting the devil know you can't be moved. You really can overcome any problem you may have. But in order to do so, you have to confront it first in the name of Jesus. You really can get control over your thoughts and feelings. But you must confront them first. That's how we cast down imaginations and every high thing that exalts itself against the knowledge of God. That's how we bring every thought into captivity to the obedience of Christ. (See 2 Corinthians 10:5.)

Don't put off confronting the darkness that's come into your life with the light of God. Out of denial, people often stay in their mess, hoping somehow they'll get lucky and the problem will work itself out. But it never does. The problem won't go away until you confront it, backed with the truth of the Word of God and the power of Jesus' name.

So the Gibeonites sent word to Joshua about the imminent threat. Joshua in turn mobilized the armies of Israel to confront the armies of the five kings in battle.

The moment you make up your mind that you are going to stand up against your enemies and fight, you'll find that you are no longer fighting alone. God will begin to fight for you. As the Israelites prepared for battle, God spoke to Joshua:

> Do not fear them, for I have delivered them into your hand; not a man of them shall stand before you.
>
> —JOSHUA 10:8

All hail breaks loose!

From the beginning of the battle, the armies of Israel overpowered the Amorite armies. To keep from being completely annihilated, the enemies turned and ran for their lives. But God wasn't finished fighting yet. While they were running away, He rained such big hailstones on them that more died from the hail than from the sword. The sun had begun to set before the battle was over, but God *still* wasn't finished. God made the sun stand still for another entire day until the enemy troops were destroyed and the defeat was complete.

What does that mean? Many times God will come to your defense in such a supernatural way that you won't even be able to explain how He did it. All you will know is that it began with confronting the enemy.

At the end of this battle story we read an interesting footnote:

> The whole army then returned safely to Joshua in the camp at Makkedah, *and no one uttered a word against the Israelites.*
> —JOSHUA 10:21, NIV, EMPHASIS ADDED

If a bunch of my folks had been killed by hailstones falling down out of heaven, I'd shut up, too.

All the power of heaven came to the defense of God's people because they were willing to confront their enemies. Even if every demon in hell lines up against you, it makes no difference. When you finally get ready to confront what's coming against you, God will send you all the power you need to win.

After confronting the enemy comes the next step...

CONTROL THE ENEMY

AFTER THE BATTLE was over and the enemy defeated, Joshua placed the five kings who had started the war against Joshua and God's people in a cave. Joshua brought under control the very thing that had wanted to control him.

This is an important point: You can control anything that wants to control you. Has doubt tried to control you? What about fear? Perhaps unbelief, insecurity, habitual sins or a host of other enemies have tried to rob you of the abundant life God promises. Through the power of the Holy Ghost you can control what wants to control you just as Joshua controlled the five kings in the cave. Those powerful kings tried to bind Joshua, but Joshua bound them.

Confronting the problem is important, but unless you have the problem under control, you'll have to confront it again.

I hear you knocking, but you can't come in!

We need to take the attitude that tells the devil, "I know what you're up to. You're trying to get me to lose control so you can take control. You're trying to pull me out of church and get me out of the Word. You're trying to get me mad at my spouse or at my boss or at the world. You're trying to get my mind so messed up that you can come in and defeat me. But I'm going to put on the mind of Christ. I'm going to fill my mind with the Word of God. I'm going to be in control. I hear you knocking, but you can't come in!"

If more Christians would respond like that, they wouldn't suffer so many defeats. When the devil tries to get you to stumble, you just make the devil aware that you know what he's up to. You know his scheme and his plan, but you are in control—not him. You're in control when you know who you are in Christ. He has placed Satan under your feet. You are positioned above him. By taking your position in Christ you render the devil helpless.

Take your position in Christ.

You're in control when you know who you are in Christ. Jesus Christ has placed Satan under your feet. As a believer, you are positioned above him. Paul prayed that believers might know who they are in Christ.

> I pray that the eyes of your heart may be enlightened, so that you may know what is the hope of His calling, what are the riches of the glory of His inheritance in the saints, and what is the surpassing greatness of His power toward us who believe. These are in accordance with the working of the strength of His might which He brought about in Christ, when He raised Him from the dead, and seated Him at His right hand in heavenly places far above all rule and authority and power and dominion, and every name that is named, not only in this age, but also in the one to come.
>
> —EPHESIANS 1:18–21, NAS

This passage says that the secret of Christ's power is found in His position. It's where Christ is seated—at the right hand of God—that makes Him powerful and mighty. It's all about Christ's position. Christ is seated in heaven, and the devil is under his feet down here on earth. The devil must bow to Christ because of His exalted position.

Now that it truly exciting, but the best is yet to come. Look at the next verse if you want to feel like shouting:

And He put all things in subjection under His feet, and gave Him as head over all things to the church, which is His body, the fullness of Him who fills all in all....

But God, being rich in mercy, because of His great love with which He loved us, even when we were dead in our transgressions, made us alive together with Christ (by grace you have been saved), and raised us up with Him, and seated us with Him in the heavenly places, in Christ Jesus.

—EPHESIANS 1:22–23; 2:4–6, NAS

When you, a believer, are in Christ, you are seated there with Him, too. Christ is in you, and you are in Him. Where He is seated is where you are seated also. That means that as you take your position in Christ, not only is Satan under Christ's feet, but he is under your feet as well.

Satan has to bow to Christ. And when you are in your position as a believer in Christ, Satan has to bow to you, too! Satan knows this fact all too well, which is why he opposes you, attacks you, shuts you down and tries to keep you in sin, in the flesh or any place but standing in your inheritance in Christ.

The last thing Satan wants you to know is who you are in Christ. He knows that if you ever figure that out, he's finished.

Who you are in Christ includes where you are positioned. Christ has placed Satan under your feet, and you are positioned above him, seated with Christ in heavenly places.

When the devil comes against you, declare before

heaven that you are taking your place as a believer. Say, "Lord, I take my position in You. You have put the devil under my feet. I walk on principalities and powers, and I'm not injured." (See Luke 10:19.)

Then look right at the devil and command that he bow before the Christ who is in you. He has no choice but to obey.

> *By taking your position in Christ, you render the devil helpless.*

Are you overwhelmed with fear? Tell the devil to bow! Are you sick with worry over your children's future or over the electric bill that you cannot pay? Tell the devil to bow! Have people come against you at work, trying to reinvent who you are by destroying your good name through slander and gossip? Tell the devil who is motivating those people to bow! Is sickness and disease attacking your body or the health of your loved ones? Tell the devil to bow! All the devils and demons of hell cannot rise against you if you don't allow them. You are in control.

Rise up and stand strong in your position in Christ. By taking your position in Christ, you render the devil helpless.

So Joshua said, "We're going to control the enemy and put them in a cave." First, you confront the enemy. Next, you control the enemy. Then comes the third key…

CONQUER THE ENEMY

SOON AFTER PLACING the enemy in a cave, Joshua returned and brought the five kings back out to finish the job.

Confronting and controlling your enemy is not enough. Unless you conquer him, he will try to come back sooner or later to conquer you. That's why you need a complete and total victory over pornography, drugs, abusiveness, anger, jealousy or any other decision Satan has made concerning your life.

So many Christians think, either consciously or subconsciously, *I gave my heart to Jesus, but there's one area in my life I want to save just for me.* Every Christian wrestles with secret sins and struggles. It may be lust or fear. It may be worry or pride. But unless it is confronted, controlled and conquered, it will come back to conquer you.

We're not playing games. There's a real heaven and a real hell. We battle against a real devil, but we also serve a real God. And the stakes we're playing for are life and death. If we don't take authority over the devil in the name of Jesus, Satan will try to destroy us.

You don't have to live in constant fear of what the devil is going to do to you. The devil's power *is* limited. Only God is all-powerful. The devil only has the measure of influence in your life that you give him through your emotions, actions and whatever you feed into your spirit (i.e., movies, television, music, the Internet or anything else you set before your eyes or listen to with your ears). That's why you need to conquer your enemy.

Joshua brought the five kings out from the cave, laid

them on the ground before the captains of his army and told the captains to put their feet on their enemy's necks. He looked his men in the eyes and then told them, "Do not be afraid, nor be dismayed; be strong and of good courage, for thus the LORD will do to all your enemies against whom you fight" (Josh. 10:25).

Here is the lesson Joshua was telling his men: "Take a really good look at what the Gibeonites were so afraid of. When it comes to the power of God, they're nothing!" Then the men slew the five kings.

Can you imagine what this experience did to the Gibeonites? After this episode, they must have felt invincible. They had witnessed the mighty power of God coming to their defense, raining hailstones on their enemies and completely destroying the authority of those who stood against them. If they hadn't been completely committed to God's cause before, they were now.

> *As you confront, control and conquer the enemy—even in only one area of your life—you will cause reverberations in the heavenlies that make the devil want to turn around and run.*

Can you imagine the reverberations this supernatural victory caused throughout the surrounding nations? If they hadn't been afraid before, they certainly were now because they knew they were no match for the God of Israel.

You don't have to be intimidated and manipulated by the devil. You have the right, the ability and the authority to reverse every decision he has made for your life. As you confront, control and conquer the enemy—even in only one area of your life—you will cause reverberations in the heavenlies that will make the devil want to turn around and run.

In the next section, we're going to look closer at *how* the believer can be fully equipped to do to the devil what God and the armies of Israel did to the armies of the five kings.

SECTION II
THE BELIEVER'S RESPONSE

Chapter 5

Never Submit to Satan's Grave

THE DEVIL IS a murderer. He not only wants to kill you, but he wants to throw you into a grave and seal it shut forever—just as he tried to do to Jesus. But I've got good news for you: You don't have to submit to Satan's grave. Jesus rolled away the stone for Himself and for you, too! Let's take a look.

The devil thought his decision had succeeded. Jesus had been falsely accused, beaten, whipped and nailed to a rugged cross on a hill overlooking Jerusalem. From a distance, bystanders watched Him writhing in agony and shouting to His Father.

Following His death, Jesus' body was laid in a tomb owned by Joseph of Arimathea, an influential leader in the community.

The next morning, Jewish religious leaders reminded Pontius Pilate of the pronouncement Jesus had made before He died: "After three days, I will rise from the dead."

"Pilate, you need to secure that tomb at least until the third day so Jesus' disciples don't steal His body and then claim, 'Jesus rose from the dead.'" The leaders continued, "If that happens, you'll have more trouble on your hands than you did before."

Pilate answered, "You're right. I'll give you some soldiers to guard the tomb. Just make sure it is sealed and completely secured." With that, the relieved chief priests and Pharisees departed and followed Pilate's orders.

On the third day, just as the sun was beginning to light the morning sky, Mary Magdalene and Mary, the mother of James, walked to the tomb to apply burial spices to Jesus' dead body. By the time they arrived, the stone that sealed the tomb had been rolled away, and sitting on the enormous rock was an angel!

Matthew 28:2 describes it this way:

> And behold, there was a great earthquake; for an
> angel of the Lord descended from heaven, and
> came and rolled back the stone from the door, and
> sat on it.

The guards Pilate had stationed were lying on the ground, obviously in shock. The angel sitting on the stone told the women, "You won't find Jesus here. He rose from the dead, just as He said He would. Now go tell His disciples that He has risen from the dead!"

Three days earlier, the religious leaders obtained permission to station guards around the tomb and seal it with an immovable stone. Now, the angel was sitting on it! Jesus overturned the stone and with it, the devil's decision. Stones couldn't even stop Jesus!

In the previous section, we looked at the nature of our enemy: The devil strips us, wounds us and abandons us. He tries to convince us to abide by his lower court decision that creates only more defeat and discouragement. When we *do* decide to follow Jesus, all hell literally breaks loose against us.

In this section, we are going to look at the overall response of the believer in reversing the devil's decision.

JESUS' TWO ENEMIES

ON THE DAY He was crucified, Jesus faced two enemies who stood between the cross and His resurrection. Those enemies were death and the grave. Death arrived Thursday evening; afterward the grave tried to hold Him in the tomb.

Many people have mixed these two foes together, assuming they were the same battle. But they were two distinct enemies that came against Christ to limit and destroy Him. Each of us will meet these enemies as well.

On the one hand, Jesus submitted to death. The apostle Paul wrote, "[Jesus] humbled Himself and became obedient to the point of death, even the death of the cross" (Phil. 2:8). Because dying on a cross was a painfully slow ordeal—sometimes lasting as long as nine days—Roman soldiers would often break the criminals' legs. Without the ability to support their weight, the strain from their outstretched arms applied pressure to their lungs, causing them to suffocate quickly. We know Jesus submitted to death because the Bible tells us that no bones in His body were broken. (See John 19:36.) Jesus willingly gave Himself to die.

JESUS REFUSED TO SUBMIT TO THE GRAVE

ON THE OTHER *hand, Jesus refused to submit to the grave.* Once He was dead, Jesus was placed in a tomb that was sealed tightly to guarantee that no one would be able to get in or get out. Roman soldiers guarded it around the clock so it would be doubly secured.

The religious leaders, and ultimately Satan, went to amazing lengths to keep Jesus locked up in the tomb. Conventional wisdom said this closed the final chapter on Jesus' life. But we know better.

> *The greater the power within you, the greater the artillery the devil uses against you.*

This demonstrates a very important lesson: the greater the power within you, the greater the artillery the devil uses against you.

YOUR POTENTIAL AND THE DEGREE OF YOUR ATTACK

I TOUCHED ON this in the previous chapter, but now I want to explain it more fully. There is a direct relationship between your potential and the degree of attack you experience.

The enemy doesn't need to bother using a high-powered machine gun on a baby Christian. All it takes is a crabby mood, a bad attitude or somebody not smiling at them to get them to stumble.

But when a Christian is seasoned and mature, the

enemy adjusts his artillery according to the potential of the person he's going after. The greater the calling and anointing upon that person's life, the greater the attack. The greater the attack, the greater the anointing.

> *The greater calling and anointing upon that person's life, the greater the attack. The greater the attack, the greater the anointing.*

Please understand that when you pray, "Lord, anoint me, use me, saturate me, set me aside and raise me up," you are also setting yourself up for an even greater level of resistance from the enemy.

A baby Christian doesn't threaten the powers of hell like a mature, Spirit-filled believer who walks by the Spirit, quotes the Word of God, knows who He is in Christ and understands how to use his spiritual armor. If you were the devil, you'd be concerned, too! Nothing scares the devil more than your potential being put to use.

If I can communicate anything to you in this chapter, it's this: The enemy is well aware of the great potential that exists in you.

You may not even be fully aware of your potential— but the devil is painfully aware of it. You might not even be saved. You might not even be committed to the Lord yet. But the devil knows that if God's mark is on you and you ever get a hold of that potential, then you're going to destroy him. He knows that once you commit—*really* commit—your life to Christ, you're going to be a force to reckon with.

> *The enemy is well aware of the great potential that exists in you.*

Because of this, he will reinforce the guard watching over your grave to make sure you never get out from beyond the stone.

The devil's decision for your life is to keep you in a state of deadness and separation from God. He knows that if you ever get up out of that grave, he is going to be in trouble.

As you grow in maturity, the battles become more intense. That's why after a spiritual breakthrough you often face even greater struggles. The devil gets fearful and tries to steal the fruit God has produced in your life.

NEVER SUBMIT TO THE GRAVE

EVERY BELIEVER IS called to take up his cross. Each one of us must submit to death; we die to our selfish desires, to our own agendas, to living for ourselves and getting our own way. But the grave is another story. Never submit to the grave!

Satan's decision in defeating Jesus involved putting a stop to Jesus' ministry. He also intended to put a stop to the ministry of Jesus' followers, too. Satan placed a stone over the tomb to stop Jesus and to stop you. The stone served three purposes:

1. To render you hopeless

Satan wants a stone rolled in front of your tomb that

is so big you will lose all hope of divine intervention.

Any time we wrestle with something that's bigger than we are, that's blocking us or that's intimidating us, our first temptation is to feel a sense of hopelessness. We begin to doubt that our situation will ever change.

Immediately following the crucifixion, Satan said to himself, "I don't believe Jesus is going to get up from that grave. But if He does, I want Him locked in so that He can never get out. I don't believe anyone is going to come in and remove His body. But if they do, I want them to feel so intimidated by the stone, the guards and the seal on the tomb that they will give up." Satan's goal was to destroy faith.

2. To render you helpless

Satan said to himself, "Now that Jesus is dead, I'm going to put a big stone in front of the tomb and place guards all around it to guarantee He stays dead! I'm going to have that tomb so well secured that anyone with any hope in the power of resurrection will feel completely helpless."

Have you ever noticed that often after people commit or rededicate their lives to Christ, they lose their job, get sick or encounter some other hardship? It's because Satan has rolled a stone in front of them. He wants to render them helpless and stop them from experiencing the resurrection or power of God's Spirit.

Satan wants you and every other believer to sit quietly in the grave, get depressed and do nothing because he's afraid that you might begin to walk in the power of new life in Christ. He would rather that you sit in the darkness and think about the past than look to the hope of your future in Christ.

The religious leaders didn't mind the disciples talking about what Jesus did in the past. They just didn't want any new miracles taking place. The devil doesn't mind you worshiping something that *used* to be or remembering what Jesus *used* to do. He is afraid of what Jesus can do through you *today!*

Satan placed a stone between death and life because he doesn't want you crossing over into a real experience with God. He doesn't want you to have an experience that changes you from the inside out, activating you rather than rendering you helpless and dormant.

The purpose of the stone was to render you hopeless, helpless and to defeat you in one more way.

3. To isolate you from your support

The religious leaders wanted to make sure no one would be able to get to Jesus while He was still in the tomb.

Have you ever noticed that when a stone is rolled in front of you you feel lonely? You begin to wonder if anyone even cares. The natural tendency among people who face hopeless, helpless situations is to isolate themselves from the very people who can help them. And worse, they tend to isolate themselves from God. But if you isolate yourself, then you are only setting yourself up to be picked off by the enemy's sniper fire without anyone to rescue you.

THE STONE IS A SETUP

THE STONE DOESN'T have to be a setup for you alone. It can also be a setup for the enemy. Every grave experience is a setup for God to intervene in your life.

> *Every grave experience is a setup for God to inter-vene in your life.*

God loves to place His children in the position where the only way out is through divine intervention. Only then is *He* positioned to receive all the credit.

God will not intervene in our lives as long as we are trying to help Him. Only when we stop trying to make something happen do we create an atmosphere for God to blow apart the stone that seals our graves.

Even people who want to rescue us can stand in God's way. We need encouragement from our brothers and sisters in Christ when we face grave situations. But we must be very careful not to look to them as our salvation. Our deliverance doesn't depend upon people, circumstances, the economy or our jobs. Our deliverance rests on God's resurrection power.

You will never experience true faith as long as you can find an exit door to escape your problems. Faith is perfected in you when you have no way out but God. If we can, we will always take the way out rather than believe God. Often God places us in impossible situations so He can show us how strong He really is. The Bible teaches that power and might will fail us: "Not by might nor by power, but by my spirit, saith the LORD of hosts" (Zech. 4:6, KJV).

Sometimes we need to be backed into a corner before God is ready to intervene. When God is in your life, if nobody comes to rescue you from the *outside*, you have enough power on the *inside* to break out of the grave. In fact, the Rock inside of you is far stronger than any rock outside of you.

> *The Rock inside of you is far stronger than any rock outside of you.*

Have you ever gone through a storm and didn't have anything to hold on to except the Rock inside of you? You looked out and you saw a rock in front of you, but you looked in and saw another Rock inside of you. I'm so glad that Jesus Christ, the Solid Rock, lives inside of us! When the storms are raging, let the Rock inside of you break through the rock outside of you.

THE STONE BECOMES A STAGE

WHEN WE HAVE nowhere else to turn, when we are completely sealed in the grave, then the stone becomes a stage. The very thing the enemy locked us in becomes an arena for God to show His glory. On Friday the stone was rolled in front of the tomb. But on Sunday morning, the stone was moved and the angels were sitting on it. How is that for thumbing your nose at the enemy?

Joseph, the son of Jacob, may have endured mistreatment from his brothers, slavery, false accusation and wrongful imprisonment, but in the end he was elevated to second in command in Egypt. His refusal to give up allowed him to save the lives of his family and continue God's promise of faithfulness to His chosen people. What the devil intended for evil, God made for good. (See Genesis 50:20.)

Even sickness can be an opportunity to be a witness of God's grace and mercy to those around you. Unemployment, family difficulties, financial struggles and every other problem you encounter can be a stage for people to see "Christ in you, the hope of glory" (Col. 1:27). The greater the stone, the greater the stage.

> *The greater the stone, the greater the stage.*

At any point Jesus could have stepped off that cross and called a host of angels to come to His aid. But He didn't. Why? He was setting up the stage for the world to see Him rise from the dead.

The Roman soldiers knew Jesus was dead; the Jewish religious leaders knew He was dead. Everybody knew He was dead because many of them had witnessed the crucifixion. Jesus' disciples knew He was dead because they had to remove His body from the cross, wrap Him in linens and place His dead body in the tomb. Then the Roman soldiers and Jewish leaders sealed the tomb just to make sure that the job was finished.

FIRST DEATH, THEN THE GRAVE

JESUS CHRIST FACED more than death. After death He

still had to face the grave. He was wrapped so tightly that He shouldn't have been able to shake off His grave clothes. And even if He arose from the dead and freed Himself of His grave clothes, how would He be able to get past the stone?

Often when we confront the devil's decision for our lives, we may conquer death but still face the grave. We're in a bad place; we're tied up, depressed, poor, busted and disgusted, but nevertheless, we're awake.

And we speak out from the grave, "Lord, I regret what I did in the past. If I had it to do over again, I would do it differently. I'm sorry about what I have said and done, but I'm awake now. Even though I've overcome death, what am I going to do about this grave?"

I have good news: If God is God enough to wake you up from the dead, then He's God enough to bring you out! The Bible says, "No weapon formed against you shall prosper" (Isa. 54:17). God *will* work it out!

> *If God is God enough to wake you up from the dead, then He's God enough to bring you out!*

When Jesus raised Lazarus from the dead, Lazarus came out of the grave still bundled up in his grave clothes. But when Jesus arose from the dead, He was so confident He could get out that He was neat. When Peter and John entered the tomb to see for themselves that Jesus was alive, the burial cloth His head had been wrapped in was neatly folded. Jesus proved He was victorious over death *and* the grave! (See John 20:6–7.)

Matthew 28:2 tells us the angel rolled the stone away from the tomb. All my life I thought Jesus was locked in and He needed the angels to get Him out. Yet John writes that Jesus suddenly appeared to the disciples despite the fact that the doors to the building were locked. (See John 20:19.) If Jesus' glorified body wasn't limited by time or space, then why was the stone rolled away?

THE REASON FOR THE STONE

THE STONE WASN'T rolled away for Jesus' benefit; it was rolled away for ours. The stone couldn't stop Jesus anymore than a door could—it was merely a platform to bring glory to God. The angel rolled away the stone and then triumphantly sat on top of it so the whole world would see that Jesus conquered death *and the grave.*

Has a devil rolled a stone in front of your grave? There is not a stone in your life that you can't get through. If you can't move it, then go through it. Greater is He that is in you than he that is in the world. (See 1 John 4:4.)

Men and women who reverse the devil's decisions for their lives understand a very important biblical principle: Stones don't stop us.

> *Stones don't stop us!*

We don't fix our eyes on the seen, we fix our eyes of faith on the unseen. (See 2 Corinthians 4:18.) We realize that every negative, difficult, hazardous situation we face is merely a public arena for God to make His power known.

We refuse to accept the devil's decision because we know that stones don't stop us.

Stones don't stop us!

Chapter 6

Better Than a Chili Dog

THERE ISN'T ANYTHING I love more than a chili dog. When I'm preaching and it gets near lunchtime, my sermons can often begin to take on food illustrations. There's nothing like feeding your powerful hunger a chili dog piled high with chili, onions and sauce—except, of course, feeding your spirit man with God's powerful Word. Let's take a look at how feeding your spiritual hunger with God's Word can equip you to reverse the devil's decision in your life.

One day, while walking along the banks of the Jordan River, Jesus stopped to watch His cousin John baptize people who were renewing their commitment to God. Sensing that His time had come to move into public ministry, Jesus offered Himself to be baptized. At first John hesitated, but after some gentle coaxing he relented.

While He was still submerged under the water, Jesus

sensed something inside activating His spirit. Emerging from the water He was immediately sensitized to the spirit world around Him. He could identify the thoughts and intentions of the bystanders on the banks of the river. And he could discern the subtle workings of His enemy, the devil.

Then, as He stood in the water, the Holy Spirit in the form of a dove appeared from high in the clouds and landed on Him. God was confirming to Him the new direction His life would be taking. Then a voice boomed out from the heavens, "This is My beloved Son, in whom I am well pleased" (Matt. 3:17). The people standing around were astonished. After thirty years of preparation, Jesus was now ready to launch into ministry.

Stepping back onto the river bank, Jesus sensed the Holy Spirit leading Him into the wilderness. There was one final test before He was to begin His ministry.

Walking through the desert, Jesus sought God's heart regarding the task that lay before Him. He spent time in the presence of His Father, knowing that over the next three years He would give everything He had to bring salvation to the world. By the end of the forty days, because He had fasted from food and water the entire time, Jesus' body was weak.

Suddenly Satan appeared. Unless he could derail God's plans for Jesus' life, Satan knew that his evil plans would be doomed. The devil decided to trick Jesus into forfeiting God's purpose for His life.

Knowing that Jesus was famished and near starvation, he pointed to some nearby rocks and said, "Jesus, if You really are the Son of God, then why don't You just turn some of these stones into bread?"

Jesus may have been hungry, but He was not about to use God's power for His own benefit. Jesus answered with a passage from Deuteronomy 8:3, "It is written, 'Man shall not live by bread alone, but by every word that proceeds from the mouth of God'" (Matt. 4:4).

Unsuccessful at his first attempt, the devil escorted Jesus to Jerusalem and stood with Him on the pinnacle of the Temple:

> …and said to Him, "If You are the Son of God, throw Yourself down. For it is written: 'He shall give His angels charge over you,' and, 'In their hands they shall bear you up, lest you dash your foot against a stone.'"
>
> —MATTHEW 4:6

Satan was tempting Jesus to perform a miracle simply to impress the Jews—without responding to human need or directing the glory to His heavenly Father. This time, however, Satan had reached into his bag of tricks and used Scripture to justify his temptation—Psalm 91:11–12. Undeterred by the devil's manipulation, Jesus answered back with Deuteronomy 6:16, "You shall not tempt the LORD your God."

Finally, the devil brought Jesus to a high mountain where they could see into the distance for miles. "If you bow down and worship me, I will give you all the kingdoms of this world."

"Away with you, Satan!" Jesus answered. "For it is written, 'You shall worship the LORD your God, and Him only you shall serve'" (Matt. 4:10).

With that, Satan departed for a short while.

On all three occasions Jesus proclaimed the Word of

God instead of arguing with the devil. The Word of God strengthened Him to stand against the temptation of the enemy even though He was worn out from going forty days without food and water.

This passage contains a key for reversing the devil's decision. If Jesus, the Son of God, needed the Word of God, how much more do we? The Word of God is essential in reversing the devil's decision for our lives.

A Malnourished Spirit

> Hope deferred makes the heart sick, but when
> the desire comes, it is a tree of life.
>
> —Proverbs 13:12

When the Bible refers to the heart of a person, it isn't necessarily referring to the organ that pumps blood through the body, but rather the spirit of that individual. Our spirits govern everything within us that is unseen—hurts, emotions, intentions, thoughts and our relationship with God.

So when you read, "Hope deferred makes the *heart* sick," it is saying, "Hope deferred makes the *spirit man* sick." But in order to make the spirit man well, we need to feed it with the Word of God.

When Jesus was hungry and His body was weak, He was tempted to turn the stones to bread. But Jesus knew where nourishment for the spirit comes from. He responded to Satan's first temptation by answering, "'Man shall not live by bread alone, but by every word that proceeds from the mouth of God'" (Matt. 4:4).

A primary key to reverse the devil's decision is to build up your spirit man.

> *A primary key to reverse the devil's decision is to build up your spirit man.*

Our society is out of control when it comes to feeding the flesh man, or the natural man. We eat beyond full, and then we want more. As a result, we are among the most obese people in the world.

Entertainment and leisure have become our chief pursuit. We go to the movies and cheer for people who engage in adulterous affairs. Some say that up to one in three men access pornography on the Internet. The American motto is rapidly becoming, *If it feels good, baby, do it!*

Modern psychology tells us to be true to ourselves, to pursue what is best for us. Yet living selfishly does nothing to fill that aching hunger inside for something that satisfies. In fact, feeding the flesh only yields death. The apostle Paul wrote, "For if you live according to the flesh you will die; but if by the Spirit you put to death the deeds of the body, you will live" (Rom. 8:13). Living according to the flesh actually plays into the devil's decision for our lives because it yields death rather than life.

Unfortunately, the church often reflects the plight of society. Our flesh is full, but our spirits are malnourished. To replenish our hope, to bring life back to our spirits, we need to infuse them with the Word of God.

OUR INPUT
DETERMINES OUR OUTPUT

JESUS SAID IN Matthew 12:35, "A good man out of the good treasure of his heart brings forth good things, and an evil man out of the evil treasure brings forth evil things."

If we feed our hearts with good things, then out of our hearts will proceed good things. When we feed our spirits with God's Word, the blessings of God's Word will be manifested in our lives. But when we feed fleshly desires that malnourish our spirits, we can expect nothing less than fleshly manifestations that leave us hungering for more.

> *When we feed our spirits with God's Word, the blessings of God's Word will be manifested in our lives.*

That is why if you build up your spirit man, you experience good things. You wonder why things are messy in your life. Your spirit man is malnourished.

Our spirits function like a creative computer. Whatever we program into it will determine what becomes manifest in our lives. Garbage in, garbage out. Blessing in, blessing out. If you want to enjoy God's blessings in your life, then you have to program your computer with the Word of God.

The problem is, most people do nothing to nourish their spirits. They stumble around Monday and Tuesday, feed their flesh and neglect their spirit, living only for themselves. Then they drag into church on Sunday morning all blurry-eyed. They sit in the pew and wonder why they don't get anything out of the sermon. It's because their spirit man is not only malnourished but on the brink of starvation.

Interestingly enough, when this happens, these individuals usually place the blame on everyone and everything except the programmer of the computer!

The choir doesn't seem to sing with the same anointing that it did in 1993. The preaching just doesn't seem as good as it was in 1993. Why do you feel that way? It's because your spirit man was alive in 1993. You were feeding on the Word of God, listening to sermon tapes and doing whatever you could to feed your spirit.

Are you wondering why you don't love Jesus as you did before? Why you struggle with discouragement or live in defeat? Perhaps you aren't feeding the Word of God into your spirit. We cannot afford to feed our spirits with negative, evil and death-giving things. When we do, we can only expect negative, evil and death-giving results. It's a spiritual law.

OUT OF THE ABUNDANCE OF THE HEART...

IN MATTHEW 12:34, Jesus said, "For out of the abundance of the heart the mouth speaks." As you program your spirit with the Word of God, you will begin speaking it. What comes out of your mouth will determine whether you live in victory or defeat.

> *What comes out of your mouth will determine whether you live in victory or defeat.*

- To reverse the devil's decision, you must *know* the Word of God.

- To reverse the devil's decision, you must *feed* your spirit with the Word of God.

- To reverse the devil's decision, you must *confess* what the Word of God says.

Your faith will never rise above what you speak out of your mouth. You will never believe for more than what you speak. You can read about faith and sing about faith, but it will never exceed your confession. If you are going to reverse the decision of the devil, you are going to have to declare and proclaim what the Word of God says.

> *Your faith will never rise above what you speak out of your mouth.*

You can't speak the Word on Sundays and then fill your heart and mouth with worldly, negative critical and vulgar words for the rest of the week. You can't even afford to take one day off. This has to be something you proclaim every day.

Make the Word of God your habit; feed on it, meditate on it and speak it because in it we find victory, health, provision and hope.

Most people never reverse what the devil is trying to do in their lives because they don't have a confession of faith. When we unite our faith to God's will and His Word, we tap into a power that reverses the devil's decision every time. Because of the power resident within God's Word, we always have hope!

GOD'S WORD BRINGS HOPE

LET'S GO BACK to Proverbs 13:12:

> Hope deferred makes the heart sick, but when
> the desire comes, it is a tree of life.

Hope deferred makes the heart sick or causes the spirit to malfunction. In the last chapter we saw that one of the devil's primary objectives is to render you hopeless. He wants you to feel there is no hope for your body. No hope for your finances. No hope for your children. No hope for you. You might as well just learn to exist and take whatever life gives you.

But that is not what my Bible says. When your hope has been destroyed, not only is your heart sick, not only has your spirit been crushed, but your outlook is affected. Your future appears increasingly dismal.

SPEAKING GOD'S WORD ESTABLISHES HOPE

THE DEVIL DOESN'T want you to know you have a future because if you knew what it was, you would no longer feel hopeless. But when you have fed your spirit with the Word of God and have made it the confession of your mouth, you can stand up to the enemy in the middle of a storm and declare to him, "No! I am not hopeless! Jeremiah 29:11 declares that I have a future and a hope! Based on the authority of the Word and name of Jesus, I declare to you that regardless of what people say or what you say, my future is bright, my hope is great, and my life is anointed with the power of God."

You may be thinking, *But you don't understand how hopeless my situation is.*

Your declaration of faith isn't based on your present condition; it's based on your future. Your future is where God is ready to take you in the name of Jesus.

> *Your declaration of faith isn't based on your present condition; it's based on your future.*

Because of God's good plans for our lives, the devil wants our future to look dismal. He wants us to feel hopeless, helpless and isolated from our support so we become disheartened and discouraged.

God wants us so full of hope that people around us look at us and wonder, "What is wrong with that person?" God wants us to walk into the doctor's office with a smile on our face and the people inside saying, "Wait a minute. What's wrong with her? She's seeing the same doctor I'm seeing. She has the same diagnosis I have, but she still has hope in the midst of death."

We answer back:

My hope is built on nothing less
Than Jesus' blood and righteousness;
I dare not trust the sweetest frame,
But wholly lean on Jesus' name.
On Christ, the solid Rock, I stand;
All other ground is sinking sand,
All other ground is sinking sand.[1]

Many people are hopeless because they have allowed the devil's decision to take root in their hearts. They believe what they see with their eyes and hear with their ears. They've allowed past disappointments to determine their expectations for the future.

You are never going to reverse the decision of the devil as long as you linger in past hurts or build your life around disappointed expectations.

SPEAKING GOD'S WORD BRINGS VICTORY

IF WE LISTEN to the devil's lies long enough, we will continue in hopelessness. But through the Word of God, we have victory. By ourselves, we have no authority over the enemy. But Revelation 12:11 tells us that "they overcame him by the blood of the Lamb and by the word of their testimony, and they did not love their lives to the death."

The believers overcame Satan first by the blood of the Lamb. Only through the blood of Jesus, the sacrificial Lamb, are we able to stand before the enemy without spot or blemish. Satan can't point to our past transgressions because they are covered by the blood of Jesus. We overcome the accuser because we do not love our lives to the death. In other words, we're not living for ourselves;

we live for the cause of Christ and refuse to feed our flesh.

We also overcome the enemy by the word of our testimony. Our testimony is the work of God's Word in our lives. The Greek word for *word* in that verse is *logos*. One way *logos* is used in Scripture is in reference to the Word of God. Hebrews 4:12 tells us that the Word—the *logos*—of God "is living and powerful and sharper than any two-edged sword." Our testimony to God's Word in our lives brings victory.

SPEAKING GOD'S WORD MAKES US POSITIVE

KNOWING THE VICTORY we have through the blood of Jesus, the word of our testimony and our refusal to walk in the flesh, we should be very positive people. I am not talking about the world's definition of having a "positive mental attitude." That notion is based on the ideas of men.

Years ago, a great preacher told me, "If the devil can ever get you in the realm of reasoning and understanding, he'll whip you every time. The only way that you'll defeat the devil is to fight the devil in the arena of faith. In the arena of faith you can get every problem settled in the Word of God."

> *The only way that you'll defeat the devil is to fight the devil in the arena of faith.*

Why should we be positive? Because we have the Word of God. Second Corinthians 1:20 tells us *all* the

84

promises of God are "Yes" and "Amen." In other words, the promises in God's Word are affirmative and *will* be fulfilled. You can't get any more positive then that.

When the Word of God explodes in your heart, it will transform you from a hopeless, heavy-hearted person into the hope-filled, positive, creative person God wants you to be.

SPEAKING GOD'S WORD MAKES US CONFIDENT

SOME PEOPLE ACCUSE me of being arrogant when I say with Paul that "I *know* whom I have believed" (2 Tim. 1:12, emphasis added). When I say that *my* God shall provide all of my needs according to His riches and glory by Christ Jesus, a lot of people think I'm being boastful and egotistical. (See Philippians 4:19.)

They ask me, "How do you know that?"

My answer is, "The Bible tells me so."

They say, "Who do you think you are?"

"I am a child of God, the righteousness of God in Christ." (See 2 Corinthians 5:21.)

"How dare you make such an outrageous claim!"

And I respond, "I dare because Paul dared."

I know people can get unbalanced and start making Scripture say what *they* want it to say. But the devil has us so afraid of the unbalanced that we don't believe God for anything big.

Dead religion does not want you to be positive, fully persuaded or secure. Dead religion wants you pessimistic, uncertain and insecure. That's why I am not a religious man. I am a Christian man. A Christian is never without hope.

You cannot fulfill your God-given destiny and purpose when you lose hope. But through hope—hope in Christ and the hope that springs from God's Word—you can reverse the decision of the devil.

God has not destined us to live in defeat and failure. "We are more than conquerors through Him who loved us" (Rom. 8:37). But in order for us to live as conquerors, we must be positive, confident, hopeful, faith-filled people.

So when you pray, be confident, hopeful and always expect results. Don't say:

- "I asked God to heal me, but nothing has changed."

- "I asked God to save my kids, but it looks as if the devil is going to get them."

- "I asked God to save my job, but they said they are shutting down in April."

- "I asked God to increase my finances, and right after that my car broke down and my refrigerator stopped working."

Despite what you can see, stand up in the face of the devil and proclaim the Word of God in the name of Jesus. Circumstances are subject to change because the things you see are temporal.

Your job can change. Your body can change. Any of your circumstances are always subject to change. But the Word of God is unchangeable. The Holy Spirit working through God's unchangeable Word can, and will, change your life for the better.

To reverse the devil's decision for your life, watch what you eat. A healthy, consistent diet of the Word of God will enable you to walk the walk of faith that God has called every one of us to walk.

Chapter 7

Take Action

THE DEVIL IS a snake. And just like a serpent that paralyzes its victim with venom, the devil will try to shut you down so that you won't even try to fight against him. But God will show you how to take action and to break the devil's hold on you. You'll be able to point to the sign over the doorway and read it aloud to him: "E-X-I-T!" That's just what happened to four lepers in Samaria.

The devil had made his decision: The people of Samaria, Israel's capital at the time, must die. The Syrian army had surrounded Samaria, strangling the flow of incoming food and water, and then sat back to watch the city slowly starve to death. Because food was so scarce, the people inside the city gates resorted to cannibalism. Parents were even eating their own children. And all they had to look forward to was surrendering at the hands of a nation who would rape their women, kill their men, steal their possessions and destroy whatever was left. Morale was terrible. The situation *looked* absolutely impossible.

In the natural, if CNN was flying around the city reporting the news, they would announce that it was a no-win situation.

Samaria was *hopeless*—they were surrounded without the prospect of another country coming to their rescue. They were *helpless*—they were vastly outnumbered by their enemies. Last of all, Samaria was *isolated*—they were cut off from supplies and the encouragement of the rest of Israel.

At the bottom of the food chain were four lepers. Lepers, because they were considered "unclean," had no source of income except to beg donations of people walking by while they sat at the entrance of the city gate. Not allowed to dwell within the city, the men had been forced to live in huts just outside the walls and were now pinned between the city gate and the surrounding army. With the gate locked shut and supplies completely choked off, they had absolutely nothing to eat.

Evaluating their hopeless situation, they looked at each other and said, "Why are we sitting here until we die?" (2 Kings 7:3).

Praise God for thinkers!

The four men then discussed their options:

> If we say, "We will enter the city," the famine is in the city, and we shall die there. And if we sit here, we die also. Now therefore, come, let us surrender to the army of the Syrians. If they keep us alive, we shall live; and if they kill us, we shall only die.
>
> —2 Kings 7:4

The men faced three alternatives. They could try to get past the gate and reenter the city where they might find food but still either starve to death or be killed by the Syrians. They could remain where they were and suffer the same fate. Last of all, they could surrender to the enemy, risking death—but possibly being made slaves. If this happened, at least their lives would be spared and they would have food to eat.

You know the situation is bad when your best option is slavery.

The four men had three strikes against them:

1. They were suffering from leprosy.
2. They were starving to death.
3. They were on the verge of being destroyed by an enemy who was waiting for the right moment to pounce on them.

They were in a no-win situation. In the natural, they had nothing to live for, nothing to hope for, nothing to motivate them and nothing to encourage them.

When confronting the devil's decision, oftentimes you are ready to strike out. You have two strikes called and a hard fastball coming in your direction. One more strike and you're out. What do you do? Your response will determine your outcome.

The desperation of the four lepers drove them to do something. They got tired of listening to their stomachs grumble and tired of living in fear. They looked at each other and said, "Why are we just sitting here waiting until we die?"

This question was tremendously important because it brought change to a hopeless situation.

TAKING ACTION

THE REASON THIS question changed their circumstances is because it changed their *response* to their circumstances. If you are in a no-win situation and whatever you are doing is not working, I want to give you some deep, educated, philosophical advice: Change your response!

> *If you are in a no-win situation and whatever you are doing is not working, I want to give you some deep, educated, philosophical advice: Change your response!*

At some point you need to come to point zero with the devil and let him know that you are not going to sit there and die. You're sick and tired of being sick and tired; no longer are you going to sit in your house moping, complaining and feeling sorry for yourself. You have to be willing to do whatever it takes to break through whatever is holding you in.

Instead of sitting outside the city gates waiting to die, they decided, "Let's take some action."

> *You have to be willing to do whatever it takes to break through whatever is holding you in.*

Many people today are sitting in utter defeat facing the roadblocks the devil has placed in front of them, looking like a calf staring at a new gate, without ever rising to their feet and entering into the battle. It's so tragic and unnecessary.

FACING YOUR ENEMY

JUST AS THE sun was setting, the men walked into the Syrian camp to surrender. The first tent they approached was unoccupied, so they went to the next one. But that tent was empty, too. They walked through the entire camp looking for someone to surrender to, but they couldn't find anyone. Strangely enough, the enemy Israel feared wasn't even there!

Unbeknownst to all of Israel, just before the four lepers arrived, the Syrians heard what they assumed was the sound of chariots coming their direction. Thinking that Israel had paid the Egyptians and Hittites to come to their defense and that they were now outnumbered, the Syrians fled the camp and ran for their lives, leaving everything intact.

But what the Syrians heard wasn't the sound of chariots— because Israel hadn't paid the Egyptians and Hittites to rescue them. God simply intervened on behalf of His people.

Most of the time the enemy we envision in our minds is much bigger than he really is. When we step out in faith to meet our enemy, we find he's gone!

> *Most of the time the enemy we envision in our minds is much bigger than he really is.*

The doctor gives you an unhealthy diagnosis for your body, but you decide to walk by faith and not by sight. After being anointed with oil, feeding your spirit with the Word of God and declaring God's truth, you return to your doctor. Taking one look at your test results, he or she says, "I don't know what happened, but I can't find any traces of your condition." You discover that the enemy mysteriously disappeared!

Best of all, four lepers—outcasts to even their own people—were able to plunder the entire Syrian army. With all the food, clothing and gold they could ever want, they enjoyed feasting on their foe. What the devil had decided to do to God's people was overturned and transformed into a tremendous victory!

Finally, in the middle of the night, the leper's consciences began to bother them. They realized they needed to share the good news with the people of Samaria. The lepers returned to the city and reported to the gatekeepers that the siege was over. After checking out the lepers' story, the gates were thrown wide open for the people to raid the abandoned camp.

The only casualty of the people's stampede out of the city gates was a city official who originally doubted in God's ability to completely turn the situation around. He was trampled to death trying to direct traffic.

Four lepers brought deliverance to an entire city!

TRANSFORMING YOUR NO-WIN INTO VICTORY

YOU CAN CHANGE your no-win situation into victory. But in order to do that you are going to have to rise up from your circumstances—just as the four lepers did.

I believe that God is ready to do the same in our situations. He is waiting for us to get up, brush ourselves off and begin to declare boldly, "Satan, I am not sitting here until I die. I refuse to accept defeat. I am taking action, and I am going to be victorious in the name of Jesus!"

FACING ADVERSITY WITH JOY

IF THE PEOPLE of Israel had known in advance what the outcome would be, would it have changed their response? Of course it would have!

The reason we can be joyful in the face of adverse circumstances is because we can read the last chapter of God's Word and find out who wins—we do! We don't have to worry when we're on the winning side. *We are winners!* We don't have to worry because Jesus defeated our greatest enemies: death and the grave (as we saw in chapter four).

The writer of Hebrews tells us that Jesus "who for the joy that was set before Him endured the cross, despising the shame, and has sat down at the right hand of the throne of God" (Heb. 12:2). Jesus could withstand the greatest assault in human history because He knew what the end looked like.

That's why James could write:

> My brethren, count it all joy when you fall into various trials, knowing that the testing of your faith produces patience. But let patience have its perfect work, that you may be perfect and complete, lacking nothing.
>
> —JAMES 1:2–4

Looking at the two Scripture references above, can

you see the relationship between joy and trials? Joy is only proven in the fires of adversity. When we're two strikes down and the devil throws us a fastball, we can swing with confidence because even if we strike out, we *will* win the ballgame.

> *Joy is only proven in the fires of adversity.*

As followers and imitators of Christ, you and I can endure anything as long as we know the final outcome. The devil, however, wants you to think that you are in a no-win situation.

We all face situations in which we must confront the devil's decision. Whether it's kicking a drug habit, losing weight, gaining control of our anger or overcoming lust, the devil tells us, "You may be trying, but you are really in a no-win situation. You have stumbled before and you'll stumble again, so you may as well give up."

But the devil is a liar! I don't care what he says. It is never too late to get up and move forward into victory. And if all you have left is God, then you and God are a majority.

ADVERSITY IS A FACT OF LIFE

HERE'S ONE LIE of the enemy that often sets us up for disappointment: Good Christians *never* face adversity. The fact is, we all face no-win situations. Jesus said, "In the world you will have tribulation." That's one promise you can bank on. But then He concluded by saying, "But be of good cheer, I have overcome the world" (John 16:33). We face certain adversity, but we also have Jesus on our side. He already overcame all the heavy artillery the world had to throw at Him...and He *still* won!

Here's another lie of the enemy that is equally damaging: Good Christians *always* face adversity. The psalmist wrote, "Many are the afflictions of the righteous" (Ps. 34:19). Some Christians justify their sorry state of affairs with this verse. They don't feel good or righteous unless they're over their head in problems or persecution. Unfortunately, they don't read the rest of the verse: "But the LORD delivers him out of them all."

When the word *afflicted* is used, it doesn't necessarily mean sickness. It means whatever the enemy is trying to throw at you to get you to give in and throw up your hands and say, "Oh, what's the use. I'm in a no-win situation."

We will face adversity, but we also have a means of deliverance. God promises He will deliver us out of them all. Now either He will or He won't. He will either give us the victory, or we will go down in utter defeat.

We can endure hardship with joy and confidence because Jesus is the author and finisher of our faith. What He started, He *will* finish. "Being confident of this very thing, that He who has begun a good work in you will complete it until the day of Jesus Christ" (Phil. 1:6).

WE CAN REJOICE BECAUSE OUR VICTORY IS SURE

THE APOSTLE PAUL wrote:

> Now thanks be unto God, which always causeth us to triumph in Christ, and maketh manifest the

savour of his knowledge by us in every place.
—2 CORINTHIANS 2:14, KJV

Notice that Paul uses the word always. *Always* means "without exception." So without exception, I will always triumph in Christ. That is cause for rejoicing.

When you look at Paul's life, you see that he put his preaching into practice. Regardless of his situation—whether it was good or bad—Paul rejoiced in the Lord. In Philippians 4:4 he exhorted the church, "Rejoice in the Lord always. Again I will say, rejoice!" Joy seems to abound throughout the Book of Philippians despite the fact that Paul wrote it from a jail cell!

Just as Paul taught and practiced, we need to learn to rejoice always. Why? Because we know that regardless of our situation, he will always cause us to triumph. He always causes us to go from a no-win situation to certain victory.

WHY WE NEED PERSEVERANCE

LOOKING AT 2 Corinthians 2:14 again, notice that Paul uses the word *causeth*. That word implies that our triumph may not always come instantly. But if we persevere, eventually God will cause us to be victorious.

Most of us don't like the word *persevere* because we want quick fixes for everything we do. Sometimes God just delivers and POW! We get the victory over a problem. But in other times, the victory takes awhile.

Because walking in triumph may take time, you have to learn to persevere until the victory is won. In the next chapter we will look more closely at perseverance.

SOMETIMES OUR
NO-WIN IS A RESULT OF OUR MESS

GOD CAN CAUSE us to triumph even when the no-win situations we face are results of our own sins and mistakes. And some of the messes we have gotten ourselves into didn't happen overnight. We may have invested time into our bondage.

> *God can cause us to triumph even when the no-win situations we face are results of our own sins and mistakes.*

Some believers have allowed their tongues to carry on in an unrestrained manner for years. Other people have uncontrolled anger with roots that have had a lifetime to grow deep in the soil of unforgiveness.

Fortunately, God is so full of mercy and grace that He is longsuffering with us even when we cause our own messes. Any time we confess our sins, we should pick up the Word and start professing and confessing the Word. God says, "I am ready to go to work for you."

God's promised triumph does not always come quickly or easily. In fact, it rarely happens overnight. More than anything, it is a result of faith, patience and perseverance.

In the mind of God, no situation is hopeless and no one is beyond redemption or deliverance. There is no end but triumph in the name of Jesus.

GETTING UP IS
THE MOST IMPORTANT THING

SO MANY BELIEVERS are in the same place as those four lepers. They fail to see that if God is for us, no one can stand against us. (See Romans 8:31.) You may be one of them.

If you want to be a person who consistently reverses the devil's decisions for your life, you have to be willing to get up from whatever situation drags you down.

Too many people are bellyachers, gripers, fault finders and criticizers, but they aren't willing to be a part of the solution. Whining and complaining are not going to get you anywhere; they will only help you dig a deeper hole in your life.

> *Whining and complaining are not going to get you anywhere; they will only help you dig a deeper hole in your life.*

The four lepers faced a no-win situation and overcame it because they were willing to do something about their predicament. Had they stayed in their huts feeling sorry for themselves, they wouldn't have been part of the solution. In fact, because they arrived at the Syrian camp first, they had their choice of the finest goods. They hid them before sharing the good news with the people of Samaria. (See 2 Kings 7:8.) Those who get up and take action will receive a reward.

When Jesus encountered the crippled man at the pool of Bethesda, He asked him, "Do you want to get well?"

The man didn't answer Jesus' question. Instead, he gave excuses for why he was never able to get into the healing waters of the pool in time when the angels stirred them. Some people don't want to get well. They're content with abiding by the devil's decision: sickness, poverty, discouragement, hopelessness.

Then Jesus then said to him, "*Get up!* Pick up your mat and walk" (John 5:8, NIV, emphasis added). Jesus didn't extend His hand and pick him up. The man literally had to take a step of faith before experiencing the supernatural power of God.

When you encounter anything less than God's best for your life, you need to heed Jesus' command to "Get up!" Not just in the physical sense. You need to get up in the Word, get up in your determination to confront, get up in your praise, get up in your commitment, get up in your confession, get up in your attitude. Just get up! Get up in the name of Jesus and refuse the chains of the devil.

Take confidence that through God, you will do valiantly. (See Psalm 60:12.) Through your God, you shall be strong and carry out great exploits. (See Daniel 11:32.) And because of that fact, you can face any no-win situation with a smile on your face and with joy in your heart because you know—you know—who is going to win. You are!

If you are in captivity to sinful habits, that is no problem. God can turn that captivity into freedom. Even if you have suffered a setback recently, that is still no problem. God can transform the setback into triumph.

If you have stumbled or fallen, that is no problem because Psalm 37:24 says of the righteous person, "Though he fall, he shall not be utterly cast down; for the LORD upholds him with His hand."

Sometimes you fall short and make mistakes. But don't get bent out of shape; just get back up in the name of Jesus. "For a righteous man may fall seven times and rise again" (Prov. 24:16).

Pick yourself up, dust yourself off and get back on your feet. Then let God give you a fresh start and fill your mouth with laughter and your tongue with singing. He'll turn your situation around so suddenly and completely that even the heathen will be amazed and proclaim that the Lord has surely done great things in your life.

But remember this important key to reverse the devil's decision: Take action. Get up and refuse to become content with anything less than God's best for your life!

Chapter 8

Going On When Your Want to Is Gone

ENDURANCE IS LIKE a little sour-mug bulldog I once knew who seemed always to want to pick a fight with two giant bird dogs. The two big bird dogs were much larger than the one stocky, muscular bulldog, but they never could seem to beat him. No matter how many times they ganged up on him, he just kept coming back. Even when they sent him home bloody and limping, he'd growl and show his teeth as if to say, "You may knock me down, you may bite on me, you may kick me around today, but I'll be back to fight you again tomorrow."

If you just keep coming back and attacking the decision the devil has made for your life, in a matter of time you'll put the devil on the run, just as that feisty little bulldog would send those bird dogs running back underneath the porch of their owner's house. Oppression will begin to run from you. Depression will begin to run from you. The problems that used to whip you won't whip you any longer. You may not be the biggest or the best, you may not have the most money and your daddy may not be the president of the company, but because you keep coming back, you'll whip them every time!

LOOKING UNTO JESUS

THE WRITER OF Hebrews wrote:

> Therefore we also, since we are surrounded by so great a cloud of witnesses, let us lay aside every weight, and the sin which so easily ensnares us, and let us run with endurance the race that is set before us, *looking unto Jesus*, the author and finisher of our faith, who for the joy that was set before Him endured the cross, despising the shame, and has sat down at the right hand of the throne of God.
>
> —HEBREWS 12:1–2, EMPHASIS ADDED

The only way to continue when the devil has decided you should give up is to look unto Jesus. The only way to stay focused and in the right perspective is by looking unto Jesus.

That phrase "looking unto" in the original Greek gives the idea of looking away from all distractions in order to focus on one singular thing.[1]

When we look unto Jesus, we give Him our undivided attention and look away from all distractions.

Distractions are everywhere. Every day, every moment, we allow ourselves either to be distracted or to focus on Jesus. Don't focus on problems; focus on Jesus. Don't focus on people; focus on Jesus. Don't focus on rebuking the devil; focus on Jesus. We'll still have problems, but when we're looking at Jesus we go *through* them instead of getting bogged down *in* them.

WE ALL ARE TEMPTED TO GIVE UP

...who for the joy that was set before Him endured the cross.

—HEBREWS 12:2

Hanging on a cross isn't an experience that evokes thoughts of joy. Dying on a cross was one of the most cruel and painful ways a person could die. Yet while hanging on the cross, Jesus prayed for His accusers, "Father, forgive them, for they know not what they do" (Luke 23:34, KJV). He didn't feel sorry for Himself, and He wasn't angry. Why? Because Jesus focused on the joy He would experience and share with His Father and His followers when He finally defeated death and the grave.

America's slogan is becoming, "If at first you don't succeed, lower your standards." For some of us, our slogan is, "If at first you don't succeed, do it the way your wife told you to do it the first time." But to succeed in life you have to learn endurance.

We need to learn how to pull ourselves up by our bootstraps and develop a Holy Spirit toughness. Jesus said, "I have given you authority to trample on snakes and scorpions and to overcome all the power of the enemy; nothing will harm you" (Luke 10:19, NIV). We have the power of God resident within us to overturn every decision the devil has made for us, including his decision to make us give up.

> *We need to learn how to pull ourselves up by our bootstraps and develop a Holy Spirit toughness.*

Let's take off our nice, religious masks and be honest. We all face times in our lives when we would like to give up. There are times when quitting church looks good. There are times when giving up our job looks good.

There comes a time in every marriage when quitting looks good. I knew a man who was celebrating his fiftieth wedding anniversary with a woman who was a little hard of hearing. Wanting to express his affection to his wife, the husband whispered in her ear, "Dear wife, after fifty years I have found you tried and true."

"I can't understand you," she replied. "Could you say that a little louder?"

He raised his voice, "After fifty years I have found you tried and true!"

"Is that right? Well, after fifty years I'm tired of you, too!"

There are even times when giving up on God looks good. The grass is always greener on the other side of the fence. So we think, "If I was over *there* instead of over *here,* I would be happier." But if you think you have problems now, jump to the other side of the fence!

ENDURANCE MEANS ATTACKING THE PROBLEM

THE GREEK WORD for *endure, hupomone,* means "to persevere and stand one's ground against opposition."

It also includes the expectation of better things to come.[2] Sometimes the answer to your prayer won't come immediately. But the delay doesn't mean God has fallen off His throne.

Daniel prayed for twenty-one days for God to give him the interpretation of a dream. Because he refused to give up and continued steadfastly in prayer, God gave him the answer. (See Daniel 10:13.) He persevered because he expected God to come through, regardless of how long it took.

Endurance is the determination to stay with a problem until it is solved. You don't have to be the best. You don't have to be the biggest. But you do have to learn to endure if you want to overturn the devil's decision.

> *You don't have to be the best. You don't have to be the biggest. But you do have to learn to endure if you want to overturn the devil's decision.*

THE REASON TO KEEP GOING

WHEN YOU KEEP getting up into adversity's face, adversity finally has to say, "Oh no! He's back up again. He's got the Word of God in his hand. He has a testimony in his mouth. He has praise in his heart and he's coming back! Every time I think I'm about to overtake him, he gets back up again!"

Can you ever be sure when you give up that you weren't right at the doorway to your answer? There are some who quit God just days before their miracle was going to be manifested in their lives. That's like some people who go through college for four years and then drop out two or three months before graduation. That's not very smart. But it's not nearly as unintelligent as people who have hung in there, prayed and stood their ground and then all of a sudden quit just about the time that their new job was about to materialize or their children were going to come back to the Lord. You can't give up!

Satan is terrified of God's children when they're determined to keep swimming despite the fog and frigid waters. He's terrified of a Simon Peter who is willing to get out of the boat and walk on the waters of faith. Satan's not afraid of someone sitting pitifully in a pool of despair saying, "I'm in this mess because of somebody else."

You have to take the Word of God and put it right under the devil's throat and let him know, "I'll be here tomorrow, same time, same station, so just get used to seeing my face and get used to this sword sticking in your gut!"

If you were the devil and you kept getting run through with the sword of the Spirit every time you picked on a person, wouldn't you get tired of it? That first thrust may not bother you, but after the third or fourth time it could get irritating. By the fifth or sixth time, getting skewered in the same place could get downright painful. Whatever decision the devil has made regarding your life, strike back with the name of Jesus and what the Word says about that decision.

Enduring With Joy

As I mentioned in the last chapter, the apostle Paul was a joyful person despite the difficult circumstances he faced. In Colossians 1:24, he wrote that he rejoiced in his sufferings. He was a man able to endure with joy.

ENDURING HARDSHIP AS A SOLDIER

PAUL WROTE IN 2 Timothy 2:3, "You therefore must endure hardship as a good soldier of Jesus Christ." The church is not teaching people to endure hardships. Our society in general avoids them. We want convenience—a life that is nice, neat, tidy and sweet. If too much is asked of us, we fold our arms together and quit.

But if the church is going to reverse the devil's decisions, we're going to have to learn to endure hardship as soldiers. There are going to be times when our lives won't make sense, when the details aren't "nice, neat, tidy and sweet." We will have times when we don't feel like going any further. But we still need to press on.

Let me remind you that we're in a fight! Many men and women in the church don't want to get in the battle; they just want to march in the military parade. And to be honest, I'd rather march in the parade, too. The parade is safe, and it requires little effort. But you don't win the war by marching in parades.

> *The parade is safe, and it requires little effort. But you don't win the war by marching in parades.*

In my home I have a picture of a young man in an impressive-looking Marine Corps uniform and a nice hat. But he only wears that uniform for getting his picture taken and for special events. When that young man is training, he takes off his uniform and puts on his combat fatigues so he can crawl around in the desert sand at temperatures that can exceed 115 degrees.

There comes a time when we have to take off our coat, hang up our dress clothes and put on the whole armor of God so we can get down and dirty when we need to get down and dirty. The military uniform looks nice, but it's not the dress blues that make us into soldiers for God. It's our willingness to put on and use our spiritual armor: girding ourselves with the belt of truth, putting on the breastplate of righteousness, shodding our feet with the preparation of the gospel of peace, taking the shield of faith, the helmet of salvation and sword of the Spirit, which is the Word of God. (See Ephesians 6:14–17.)

> *The military uniform looks nice, but it's not the dress blues that make us into soldiers for God. It's our willingness to put on and use our spiritual armor.*

When a young man or woman joins the military, his or her drill instructors do not begin by saying, "Good to see you! God bless you for being here! How are you? Just sit down if you're tired. I'm tired too, so I think I'll sit down. What? Oh, we're going to eat in just a minute. No, we won't be doing anything after that because that food's got to settle in your stomach, and we wouldn't want you to get indigestion. We're just going to rest for a few days before we begin to go into discussions about military tactics. Would you excuse me for a minute while I help that person get off the bus?"

Yet that's the way we want the Lord to deal with us. We expect Him to look down from heaven and say, "Don't you worry about getting to church this Sunday. I know how busy and tired you must be. You just stay home and rest. Don't worry about coming to Wednesday night service—I know you need the family time. And if you feel that you don't need to tithe in the summer, that's all right. You have a vacation coming and you could use that money to stay a few extra nights and put a little more gas in your boat. You need a break. You what? You want to take a two-month break from the choir? That's fine. You just do what you want to do. Oh, and don't worry about taking your turn in the nursery. Who wants to be back there with those loud kids? After all, you've hung in there for six months, and you need a break."

When you join a real army, the moment you step off that bus, the drill instructor starts screaming at you. If you mention your momma or taking a break they'll knock you upside your head. "Momma? What do you mean? I'm your momma from now on!" "You want a break? I'll give you a break. You just start running, and when I tell you to stop, then you can take a break."

Do you know why the drill instructor is so harsh? Because he knows that if he's nice and sweet he'll do nothing to prepare you for a real war. He knows he needs to toughen you up. It works the same way in God's army. God knows that when you get out and the battle gets heated and you want to give up and somebody in the youth group is depending on you, that your training will give you the ability to hang in there. He wants to toughen you up so you endure until the cancer is gone, until the arthritis goes out of your body or until your kids come home.

God is looking for men and women who will hang tough come hell or high water. He wants soldiers who will fight and not flee in the heat of the battle. God is at work preparing believers who will persevere until the manifestation comes!

> *God is at work preparing believers who will persevere until the manifestation comes!*

There are a lot of people in the house of God who love comfort. You can't build great works for the glory of God with people who are soft. Hebrews 12:7 says, "Endure hardship as discipline; God is treating you as sons. For what son is not disciplined by his father?" (NIV). Hardship and discipline are proof that you're in the family of God. He'll work you over a little bit, but He'll also help you to be better. A quitter never loses graciously. He's just a loser. When you encounter trials, thank God for them because you'll never grow if you never have any resistance in your life.

CHOOSING TO ENDURE

ENDURANCE IS A decision, not a feeling. When you run into hardships, don't expect some angelic being to fly down from heaven and touch you and give you a supernatural dose of endurance. You choose whether or not you're going to endure.

Even at a young age he made the choice to endure. He

spoke with a lisp, and as a result, he was ridiculed by his peers. When he was sixteen, his teacher wrote on his report card, "a conspicuous lack of success." His pursuit in higher education was difficult, and his grades never indicated that he would disprove his teacher's earlier evaluation. When England, his native country, entered a war, he was rejected from enlisting in the military because they said, "We need *men*."

He pursued a life in politics, and once when he stood to address his colleagues in the English House of Commons, they all walked out. He often spoke to empty chairs and echoes. At age sixty-six, he was selected to serve as prime minister and form a new government after the previous prime minister's efforts failed at stopping Adolf Hitler and his Nazi regime. Once in office, he announced to the Germans, "We're never going to give in. We're going to win the victory." Rising out of relative obscurity, his brilliant leadership and dogged determination enabled England to stand against Adolf Hitler and Nazism.

Toward the end of his storied life, this famous man—Winston Churchill—was asked to give the commencement address at a British university. By this time he was physically unable to walk on his own, so he was helped to his place. As he stood at the podium looking over the wide-eyed crowd—young men and women with their lives ahead of them—he paused and then gave one of the shortest but most memorable speeches of the twentieth century. This is what he said:

Never give up. Never give up. Never give up.

Winston Churchill turned around and hobbled back to his seat. For a seemingly long period of time there was silence. Then one by one people began clapping. Like an approaching rain shower, the peals grew louder and louder until it intensified into a deafening storm of applause. The people stood to their feet and honored the man they knew practiced what he preached.[3]

Winston Churchill was a man of true endurance. Countless times he could have given up, but because he continued forward with dogged determination, he overcame all the obstacles that stood before him. That's how we need to be in the spiritual realm.

Not every race is won on the first lap. But if we continue forward and focus on Jesus rather than the circumstances at hand or the devil's decision, we *will* come out victorious.

Chapter 9

Pursuing the Unseen

S OME PEOPLE THINK faith frees them from responsibility. If that were true, I could write a note on our
church's whopping electric bill, "Jesus paid it all."

Such things actually happen. For instance, once a
man tried to buy a motor home from a car dealership.
Where the application asked for the amount of the
down payment, the man wrote, "My father owns the
cattle on a thousand hills."

The salesman at the motor home dealership looked
at the man's answer on the application and told him,
"When you sell a cow, come see me."

This man thought he was taking a step of faith to try
to purchase a motor home without money. But the one
taking the biggest step of faith would have been the
motor home dealership. If the man defaulted on his
loan, the dealership would suffer the greater loss.

THE IMPORTANCE OF FAITH AND PATIENCE

FAITH AND PATIENCE stand between us and the fulfill-
ment of God's great and precious promises for our
lives. Hebrews 6:12 tells us, "We do not want you to
become lazy, but to imitate those who through faith and
patience inherit what has been promised" (NIV). If the
devil can undermine our faith and wear down our
patience, he can prevent us from inheriting everything
God has promised us.

In this chapter and the next I will address the role
faith and patience play in reversing the devil's decisions.

THE IMPORTANCE OF FAITH

IT'S AMAZING TO me how so many Christians under-
emphasize the importance of faith. Faith just isn't a big
deal to them. In fact, to many the subject is boring. Yet
so much of what we do as Christians is exercised by
faith in God.

- We're saved by faith.
- We're healed by faith.
- We receive the infilling of the Holy Spirit by faith.
- We believe Jesus is coming again by faith.

"But without faith," we read in Hebrews 11:6, "it is
impossible to please Him, for he who comes to God
must believe that He is, and that He is a rewarder of
those who diligently seek Him." Every Christian
believes that God exists, but far too many fail to realize
that He also rewards those who diligently seek Him.
Men and women who walk by faith experience the
blessings that follow faith. So if you want to enjoy

God's benefits and God's blessings, you need to be a person of faith.

People say, "I don't want to be a part of the Faith Movement." But without faith in God and His Son Jesus, you are bound for hell and a pawn of the devil's whims. Faith is the lifeblood of the believer. Without it, you simply *cannot* live.

WHAT IS FAITH?

FAITH IS LIKE electricity or like the wind. You cannot hold it in your hand. You cannot see it in a jar. You cannot package it in a box. Yet faith is a *substance*. The Bible says, "Now faith is the substance of things hoped for, the evidence of things not seen" (Heb. 11:1). You may not be able to see your son or daughter saved in the natural, you may not be able to see the finances you need in the natural, but in your spirit you can see them as a reality.

Faith is the assurance that what is real in the unseen will be made real in the seen. As believers, what we believe for by faith in our hearts is as real as what we can see with our eyes or feel with our hands. Why? Because faith is a substance, a rock-solid assurance. In the realm of faith anything can happen if we will believe what the Word of God says.

> *The proof of faith is revealed in our pursuit of the unseen.*

We read in Hebrews 11:3, "By faith we understand that the worlds were framed by the word of God, so that the things which are seen were not made of things which are visible." People want to be able to see it to believe it. And if they can't see it, then they don't believe it. But that's not faith. The proof of faith is revealed in our pursuit of the unseen.

FAITH IS
PROVEN BY OUR WORKS

MARK TWAIN ONCE said, "Everybody talks about the weather, but no one does anything about it." People do the same with faith. We like to talk about faith, we like to read about faith, we like to hear inspiring, anointed sermons about faith, yet we are unwilling to actually step out in faith. Paul wrote, "For the kingdom of God is not a matter of talk but of power" (1 Cor. 4:20, NIV). While faith lies in the unseen, it is exercised in the arena of the seen. We must have faith, but we also must have the works that accompany faith. Not until our confession—our talk—is supported by our actions do we find God's power released.

> *While faith lies in the unseen, it is exercised in the arena of the seen.*

This is where some people have gotten unbalanced concerning the confession of faith. They say, "I confess I'm healed," yet they neglect to act on their confession.

117

They want a greater measure of faith, but they aren't willing to back it up with action.

Confession is very important. As I mentioned in chapter five, we are snared by the words of our mouth. But I also believe that we must *walk* by faith. We can speak out good things, but we must also do something.

Faith without works is like gold within the earth. It is of no value until it is mined out. And mining requires work. In James 2:17 we read that "faith by itself, if it does not have works, is dead." Faith cannot stand alone; it has to be coupled with an act—with works. One individual with faith in God and with the actions to back it up constitutes a majority over the devil's decision and any other obstacle that may stand in the way.

> *Faith without works is like gold within the earth. It is of no value until it is mined out.*

Some people spend their entire lives waiting for their ship—their needs and requests—to come in. When you ask them, "How long have you been waiting?", they answer, "Forty years."

My advice to people like that: Don't wait for your ship to come in; swim out to it! Make an effort. Pursue! Quit sitting around waiting for a ship to come by and for somebody to throw you something over the side. Thomas Edison said it best: "Opportunity is missed by most people because it is dressed in overalls and looks like work."

> *It's not enough to know that you know. It is more important to show that you know.*

Some people take a fatalistic approach to faith. They say to themselves, "It doesn't matter what I say or what I do. God is God, and He'll do it if He wants to; if He doesn't want to, He won't." No! Jesus said in Mark 11:24, "Therefore I say to you, whatever things you ask when you pray, believe that you receive them, and you will have them." Faith activates God's will in our lives. Often what holds up our answer from heaven is our unwillingness to step out in faith.

SHOW WHAT YOU KNOW

TRUE FAITH HAS hands and feet. It's not enough to *know* that you know. It is more important to *show* that you know. The word *work* appears in the Bible 564 times, so work is not a vague scriptural concept. When faith and works operate together, the result is a work of art. Faith is the divinely inspired picture in the mind of the artist, but works are the brushes that paint the masterpiece.

> *Faith is the divinely inspired picture in the mind of the artist, but works are the brushes that paint the masterpiece.*

TRUE FAITH PLEASES GOD

TRUE FAITH IS what I call the divine attention getter. Faith always stimulates incredible favor with God because faith is the magnet that attracts God toward you. Years ago, Smith Wigglesworth said that faith causes God to pass over a million people just to get to you.

Whenever you use your faith, you please the heart of God. Don't *you* appreciate when somebody trusts you? As we examined earlier in the chapter, Hebrews 11:6 says that without faith it's impossible to please God and that He is a rewarder of those who diligently seek Him. A lot of people put a period after the word rewarder. But it says you have to go on and diligently seek Him.

MOVING MOUNTAINS WITH A GRAIN OF FAITH

WHAT PREVENTS MANY people from stepping out in faith is the lack of confidence in their own faith. They say to themselves, "Unless I'm a giant of faith, my prayer won't be answered." But the good news is, you don't have to have a large measure of faith to see miracles happen. All you need is a little faith.

Jesus said, "If you have faith as a mustard seed, you will say to this mountain, 'Move from here to there,' and it will move; and nothing will be impossible for you" (Matt. 17:20). If you have ever looked at a mustard seed, you realize how small it is. God isn't asking you to start out with the faith of an Abraham or Paul. He just wants you to start somewhere.

> *God isn't asking you to start out with the faith of an Abraham or Paul. He just wants you to start somewhere.*

People say, "I'm not like my pastor. I don't have the faith that he has to believe for my healing. I'm embarrassed by my lack of faith." Every Christian is given a measure—a seed—of faith that is planted in the soil of his or her spirit. Romans 12:3 tells us, "God has dealt to each one a measure of faith." We choose, however, to allow that seed to lie dormant or to flourish and grow. No one else is responsible to cultivate the seed of faith in our lives—not our pastors, spouses or anyone else. It's up to us.

Many Christians struggle over tithing 10 percent of their income. Believe it or not, tithing is an act of faith because that 10 percent can easily go hundreds of different directions. But to give 10 percent and believe God to supply their needs on 90 percent of their income—now that's faith!

If you struggle giving 10 percent, then start smaller—like 2 percent—and work your way up as your faith increases. Start with something small before you get to something big. The key is to start getting some seeds in the ground. God doesn't need a lot to do a lot.

God wants to bless you in a far greater way than you can imagine. He is able to do "exceedingly abundantly above all that we ask or think, according to the power that works in us" (Eph. 3:20). Not only is God able, but

He's also willing! He isn't content giving you enough; God always gives an overflow. So when He blesses you back for your act of faith, it won't be in just a minute measure. It's going to be pressed down, shaken together and running over!

Many Christians fail to step out and do what God has called them to do, and as a result, their mountains never move. But if you have faith even the size of a mustard seed, then you can say to the mountain, "Move from here to there," and it will move. Jesus said that when you have the faith of even a mustard seed, nothing—nothing—will be impossible for you!

Some of the biggest mountains you face were placed there by the devil. The devil does not want you to have an overflow of blessings. The devil does not want you to get hold of the message of faith. The devil wants you stifled and stymied. He wants you beaten and pressed down. He doesn't want you to have God's best, so he'll throw every kind of mountain in front of you. But if your faith is only the size of a mustard seed, you can speak to the mountain standing in your way and say, "You've got to move because I'm moving on and I'm going to get the best that God has for me!"

You Must Pursue What You Really Believe God Wants You to Possess

THERE ARE A lot of people in church who can't make up their minds about what they want. Led by their feelings, they're like waves tossed around by every wind. One day they are confident God is going to lead them to the right job. But the next day they become discouraged and spend entire days just feeling sorry for themselves.

Like the wind, they blow one direction one day and then go the opposite direction the next.

James described these people this way:

> If any of you lacks wisdom, let him ask of God, who gives to all liberally and without reproach, and it will be given to him. But let him ask in faith, with no doubting, for *he who doubts is like a wave of the sea driven and tossed by the wind.*
> —JAMES 1:5–6, EMPHASIS ADDED

You must pursue what you really believe God wants you to possess, regardless of how you feel.

God is looking for consistent people who know who they are in Christ, who know what the Word says about every situation and who get directly in line with God's Word.

Pursuing God's promises without wavering requires faithfulness. The same Greek word for *faith,* in fact, is used for *faithfulness.* Thus, true faith means not wavering back and forth between faith and doubt. We may sense doubt rising within us, but that is why God gave us the sword of the Spirit, which is the Word of God, to strike it down.

FAITH IN THE BALANCE

FAITH DOES HAVE a balance. My son enrolled at a Bible college a few years back. When he was applying, the school sent him an application form that scrutinized everything in his life. About the only question missing was, "How long are your teeth?" Interestingly enough, at the end of the application, where the applicant is instructed about sending money, the form read, "No checks. Money orders or cashier's checks only. Don't come and say that you have a ministry."

In other words, the school had experienced problems in the past with people who enrolled by "faith." Unfortunately, when the tuition money didn't materialize as the student claimed it would, the school was left with an unpaid bill.

THREE KEYS TO INCREASING YOUR FAITH

THE DISCIPLES HAD been unable to deal effectively with a deaf and dumb spirit that was causing a boy to suffer severe convulsions, so he was brought to Jesus. After hearing an overview of the boy's story, Jesus said to the father, "If you can believe, all things are possible to him who believes" (Mark 9:23).

In utter desperation, the man cried out, "Lord, I believe; help my unbelief!" (v. 24).

How often are we like that man? We want so much to have faith, and on some days we have the faith to move mountains. But on other days we struggle with an overwhelming sense of unbelief. I'd like to conclude this chapter by giving you three keys to increasing your faith.

Key #1: Hear the spoken Word of God.

This is the most important key in increasing your faith. Romans 10:17 says, "Faith comes by hearing, and hearing by the word of God." The Word of God waters the seed of faith already residing within you. Read the Word, listen to the Word, get the Word deep inside you.

Don't just let the Word settle in your mind; let it settle in your spirit as well. As long as you only allow it to stay in your mind, the devil can convince you to reason it away. He'll tell you, "You can't ask God for that. It just won't work. The mountain is too big."

> *The Word of God waters the seed of faith already residing within you.*

You allow the Word to settle in your spirit by meditating on it, chewing it, praying it and then seeking ways to live it out. When you dissect an animal, you kill the animal. When you dissect the Word of God, you kill it, too. Don't just learn what the Word means; learn what the Word means for *you*. Don't just confess what the Word says; confess what the Word says to *you*.

Key #2: Exercise the faith you already have.

The problem we deal with is not a lack of faith. As I already mentioned, if we are Christians, we already have a measure of faith. The problem is that what faith we have isn't utilized. Like a muscle, the more we exercise it, the stronger our faith becomes. Faith causes ordinary people to accomplish the extraordinary and turns common people into uncommon achievers.

> *Faith causes ordinary people to accomplish the extraordinary and turns common people into uncommon achievers.*

If you are struggling with a problem that seems insurmountable, start small. Take smaller steps of faith, such as praying for other people who are sick or believing God to remove a smaller mountain. In fact, sharing your faith is a great faith builder because whatever we give away, God multiplies back to us. "Give, and it will be given to you: good measure, pressed down, shaken together, and running over will be put into your bosom. For with the same measure that you use, it will be measured back to you" (Luke 6:38). As you watch God using you in other people's lives, it will become easier to believe that God can move the mountains in your life.

Key #3: Be careful what you feed your spirit.

Just as feeding your spirit with the Word of God *increases* faith, we can also feed our spirits with things that *deplete* our faith. If you spend time with skeptics, you'll become skeptical, too. If you spend time with people who are full of faith, you'll become full of faith, too. Don't let anybody dump their trash into the well of your spirit. By trash I mean their gossip, slander, lust, filthy jokes, hidden agendas and their malicious campaigns against others. You don't have to be rude to them—just avoid them. There are a lot of people who would be further along in their faith, but they allow others to dump their trash in them.

By feeding godless, sin-provoking trash into your spirit, you give Satan an entry into your life to destroy your faith. If he can get a foothold through sin, you'll struggle trying to reverse the decision he has made for your life.

Faith is the foundation of the Christian life. Without it, we cannot even be saved. But when it is exercised on a consistent basis, we rise above the level of mediocrity that plagues both the non-Christian and Christian alike, and we exhibit a life of godliness and power that enables us to live like Jesus.

Chapter 10

The Answer Is on the Way

A YOUNG MAN WALKING along the shore of a large lake came upon a famous old preacher who was fishing off the side of a dock. Seizing the opportunity to spend a few moments with a man he greatly admired, the young man approached the preacher. "I want to be a great preacher like you," the young man said. "You minister all over the world, you're in great demand, people are healed and delivered wherever you speak. What does it take to be like you?"

The preacher didn't even look up from his bobber floating in the water because he didn't want to be bothered.

Oblivious to the preacher's silent response, the young man began pelting him with a steady stream of questions, "Whose books do you read? What school should I go to? How do you think a preacher ought to dress?"

After awhile, the old preacher reeled in his line and set his fishing rod down on the dock. He walked up to the young man, grabbed him by the shoulders and threw him in the lake.

Because the young man couldn't swim, he began to sink. As he furiously began flapping his arms and legs in the water, he rose to the surface. "Helpppp, I can't swim!" he gasped in between gulps of air and water. But the old preacher stared down at the helpless man, virtually emotionless.

Just as the young man was ready to give up, the preacher leaned over the edge of the dock, stretched out his hand and pulled the man toward him.

Lying on the wooden dock, alternately coughing and breathing heavily, the young man expressed his shock. "I can't believe what you just did to me! I could have drowned! I wanted to be like you, but all you did was push me in the lake and nearly kill me!"

The old preacher motioned for the man to stop and then uttered words of wisdom that would never be forgotten. "Do you remember how badly you wanted to breathe, when you thought you were going to die?" The young man nodded affirmatively. "That's how badly you have to want God."

The old man turned around, picked up his fishing pole and cast his line back into the water.

The degree of our desire determines our willingness to wait. If you only wait a few days for God to answer and then say, "Forget it. I'll do something else," then you didn't want it bad enough to get it.

> *The degree of our desire determines our*
> *willingness to wait.*

In the last chapter, we looked at the role faith plays in reversing the devil's decision. Hebrews 6:12 tells us, "We do not want you to become lazy, but to imitate those who through faith and patience inherit what has been promised" (NIV). Some people have the faith to believe in God's ability, yet they lack the patience to wait on God's timing.

We live during a period when many people in the church are talking about prayer. In books and on the radio and television, we can learn how to pray effectively so our prayers are answered.

Although we realize God is a supernatural God, that His ways are far higher than ours, we still get hung up on particular methods. We assume God must answer our prayers in the way we expect and according to our own timing. We tend to fall in love with the method of God's movement rather than falling in love with God.

Often when we are challenged to believe and pray for a need and don't experience an immediate answer, we think that something is wrong with us. As a result, what we see as a lack of response on God's part creates spiritual guilt on our parts. Evaluating what we consider a failure, our heads spin with endless thoughts and questions: *What did I do wrong? Was it something I said? Did I have enough faith?*

Interestingly enough, this self-evaluation plays right into the devil's hand. He wants us to condemn ourselves because then our focus turns toward ourselves rather than God. The devil's decision for us is to cause us to lose patience so we don't press in until the prayer is answered.

One common experience we *all* share is asking God for something and not seeing Him respond. If we live long enough and pray hard enough, we will all eventually encounter a period in our lives when we intercede for something but fail to see God's intervention. We wait and wait, yet the windows of heaven remain firmly closed. Finally, like Job, we cry out to God, "Where are You? I've looked everywhere, but I can't find You. I'm standing here in sackcloth and ashes. I've lost everything, and I'm at the point of desperation. I don't know how much longer I can wait for You to answer me. Where are You?"

THE PURPOSE OF PATIENCE

WHILE WE'RE SO easily concerned with *things*, God is concerned about *us*. While we're building houses and buildings, sending our kids to college and trying to make something out of our lives, God is concerned about building us.

Sometimes in order that *we* might be built, the answer to one of our prayers must be delayed. So that patience might have its perfect work, God puts the answer on hold and allows us to wait because waiting does much more for us than the answer.

> *God puts the answer on hold and allows us to wait because waiting does much more for us than the answer.*

It's in waiting that that you learn an important lesson: As long as you have God—even if you don't get the answer you want—you're still OK. The apostle Paul said it well: "If God is for us, who can be against us?" (Rom. 8:31).

It's in waiting that we develop a relationship with the Giver. Perhaps God delays the answer because that is His only way to get us to spend time with Him. After beseeching God innumerable times, we begin to see Him as more than just a divine Santa Claus who gives us whatever we want.

It's in waiting that our faith is made strong. If God gave us everything we wanted when we wanted it, faith would no longer be required. Faith is fostered in delay.

We have to learn how to wait on God not knowing *when* He's coming or *how* He's going to move. We must rest assured that He *will* move. We may have to wait awhile, but the good news is, God is always on time!

Entering Into Travail

Daniel was serving in the court of Cyrus the king of Persia while the Jews were in captivity to the Persians. One day while in prayer, God gave Daniel a vision of what was going to happen to Persia as well as the surrounding nations. Distressed by the vision's magnitude and uncertain about what the vision meant, Daniel recorded his response:

> In those days I, Daniel, was mourning three full weeks. I ate no pleasant food, no meat or wine came into my mouth, nor did I anoint myself at all, till three whole weeks were fulfilled.
>
> —DANIEL 10:2–3

For three weeks Daniel fervently sought God in prayer, fasting and brokenness. Yet despite doing all the right things, heaven was conspicuously silent. But still, Daniel humbled himself and entered into a state of travail, or what Daniel referred to as mourning.

Travail brings discipline to your spirit. In the travail of prayer we say to God, "Not only do I want the answer to my prayers, but I want it more than food, more than clothing, more than comfort. I need an answer so badly that I'm willing to afflict myself with fasting in order to get it."

Afflicting yourself means to place not only your body but every part of your being under subjection to your spirit. It means going without food in order to concentrate all your energies solely toward God and the need at hand. When speaking about the reason for fasting and affliction, God asked the prophet Isaiah, "Is it a fast that I have chosen, a day for a man to afflict his soul?" (Isa. 58:5).

It's interesting that the word for *longsuffering* in some versions of the Bible is translated *patience* in others. Patience means suffering long. *Affliction* and *mourning* are the willingness to enter into fasting and affliction in order to hear from God.

Fasting and affliction don't fit into popular theology, but they are very biblical. Through fasting and affliction we break through the blockages in prayer that hinder us from touching God. We pray to God, "I'm tired of listening to myself talk. It doesn't matter what I think. What matters is what You think. Now I need to hear from You, and I'm willing to go without food and other comforts to focus solely on You alone."

> *Through fasting and affliction we break through the blockages in prayer that hinder us from touching God.*

As we spend time in the presence of God, we begin to sense something rising up inside our spirits. We aren't sure what it is, but we know it's there. We don't give birth to a vision right away, because it needs time to develop. For Daniel, the progression from impregnation to birth took three weeks. For some people the period is longer, and for others the period is shorter.

Between the impregnation of God's vision and the birth of that vision stands the time of travail. You cannot have a birth without it.

God says, "I'm not going to jump at the snap of your fingers. I'm never going to be a butler or a bellhop in your life. Between the time you ask me for certain things and the time I answer, you're going to go through travail."

WAITING REVEALS THE
DEGREE OF OUR NEED FOR GOD

As we humble ourselves before God, we become broken people and prove to Him how badly we want Him to intervene. At times in our lives, God says, "I'm going to let you wait until you've proven your desire, until you say, 'Whatever it takes, no matter how long I have to wait or how much I have to cry. God, I want it badly enough to go through frustration and travail to learn patience to do what you want me to do.'"

Daniel afflicted himself for three weeks. He didn't eat, he didn't drink, he didn't shave or take a bath. He only focused on one thing: hearing from God.

He wasn't fasting to impress God or because he had tremendous will power. He simply lost his appetite for the things he used to enjoy. You would think that after a day or two of effort, God would have said something. But for twenty-one days of seeking God, Daniel didn't hear one thing! Three weeks of suffering and all Daniel heard from God was silence.

ONLY ONE PERSON GIVES BIRTH TO THE VISION

FINALLY, AN ANGEL appeared to Daniel and explained the vision.

> And I, Daniel, alone saw the vision, for the men who were with me did not see the vision; but a great terror fell upon them, so that they fled to hide themselves.
>
> —DANIEL 10:7

Have you ever been in a situation where God gave you

a vision, but nobody else around you seemed to catch it? There is no such thing as multiple people giving birth to a single baby. The only person who saw Daniel's vision is the one who afflicted himself and travailed to receive it.

After you have suffered awhile, God gives you access to privileged information that other people don't get. When you've cried in the middle of the night, you get a joy that looks fanatical to other people because they haven't experienced what you've been through.

> *After you have suffered awhile, God gives you access to privileged information that other people don't get.*

God wants to see if He can trust us with a blessing. He wants us broken in the process so He can bless us without us using the blessing to manipulate others. He wants us to sweat it out for twenty-one days before we get blessed so we aren't teaching seminars on how strong we were when we got it. He wants us telling people, "If the Lord hadn't been on my side, I wouldn't have made it. I didn't know if I was going to make it, but just when my faith failed, His faith in me continued—not through me but in spite of me."

When the blessing was ready to manifest, Daniel said, "Nobody else saw it but me. I alone saw the vision; the men who were with me did not see the vision. A great terror fell upon them, and they ran to hide."

The men around him couldn't see the angel of God, but they could feel him.

When God gets ready to exalt you, other people may not see where you are going, they might not understand, they might not have the specifics, but there ought to be some kind of witness in other believers that God is with you.

At the same time, when God gave the revelation, everyone around Daniel abandoned him.

When all the others leave you and you're gasping for life like the young man drowning in the river...when those who said, "I'll always be there," begin to act strangely...when all hell breaks loose...that's *the* sign God is getting ready to reverse the devil's decision in your life. That's *the* sign the Lord will show up and make His presence known in your situation.

WE LEARN BEST WHEN WE'RE ALONE

YOU CAN'T HEAR God's voice until everybody is gone and you're all alone. Jacob wrestled all night with God alone. Moses talked to God on Mt. Sinai alone. Jesus prayed in the Garden of Gethsemane alone.

There is no better place to get a revelation from God than at three o'clock in the morning, looking into the darkness with tears streaming down your face, crying, "God, where are You? Nobody cares. I feel abandoned."

God says, "Yes. That's where I want you—all by yourself. I wanted to talk to you while you were with all those people. I got tired of trying to get your attention, so I moved them on. Now you don't have anyone to talk to but Me."

Don't try to keep from being alone; it's part of your spiritual development. That's when you learn who God is. That's when He has a chance to get your attention.

When your spiritual reserves are exhausted and you say, "Though He slay me, yet shall I trust Him," then God says, "Now you're getting ready for the blessings of God."

When you discover you aren't anything and all you have left is God, then you're ready for a miracle.

GOD *DID* HEAR AFTER ALL!

WHEN THE ANGEL finally appeared to Daniel, he said:

> Do not fear, Daniel, for from the first day that you set your heart to understand, and to humble yourself before your God, your words were heard; and I have come because of your words.
>
> —DANIEL 10:12

The angel didn't talk about what Daniel prayed on the twenty-first day; he talked about what Daniel prayed on the first day. You see, God heard Daniel's prayer right from the beginning.

He said, "I heard you then, but I'm going to answer you now.

- "I don't want you to think I'm hard of hearing.

- "I don't want you to think that all those prayers were for nothing.

- "I don't want you to think that I didn't hear you until after you prayed twenty-one days.

- "I heard you on the first day."

When you get to the end of your test, you'll discover that what you did on the first day is just as important as what you did on the twenty-first day.

What often occurs is that by the time we reach the twenty-first day and still haven't seen any changes to our situation, the devil tells us we're not going to receive anything from God. He tries to convince us to give up.

GOD *NEVER* FORGETS

CORNELIUS WAS A centurion in the Italian regiment. Acts 10:2 describes him as "a devout man and one who feared God with all his household, who gave alms generously to the people, and prayed to God always." He faithfully served God despite the fact that we find no evidence that his prayers were ever answered. But in spite of this, Cornelius was patient and continued faithfully in prayer.

One afternoon, an angel of the Lord appeared to Cornelius and spoke to him, "Your prayers and gifts to the poor have come up as a memorial offering before God" (Acts 10:4, NIV). After giving further instructions, the angel departed, and Cornelius shared his experience with two of his servants as well as another devout soldier.

Notice the parallels between Daniel and Cornelius:

- They prayed fervently.

- They were greeted by an angel of God.

- They received a vision from God after an extended wait.

- God told them, "I heard your prayers."

- They were the only ones to receive the vision.

God heard Cornelius's prayer but didn't answer it right away. Cornelius waited on God, and God waited for the appointed time. God said, "I heard you then, but I'm going to answer you now."

You see, God never forgets. When you continue seeking Him fervently and consistently, He sees it. He may not answer you immediately, but He will when the time is right.

To reverse the devil's decision we need the faith to believe God is bigger than our problems, and we also need the patience to wait on God to bring our answer to fruition. A delay in God's response does not necessarily mean denial. It simply means a delay. In the meantime, God uses the opportunity to make us more like Himself. For that reason, there is no such thing as wasted time.

Endurance, faith and patience all play an important part in reversing the devil's decision. The last element needed to adequately equip yourself to reverse the devil's decision in your life is obedience—the subject of the next chapter.

Chapter 11

The Will to Do His Will

I WONDER WHAT WE look like to God. He speaks to His people and says, "Go tell that stranger about the gospel." Or, "Give an extra $20 in the offering plate next Sunday." So often we don't respond, don't move and don't even acknowledge His command. We stand there immobile, like a calf staring at a new gate.

If we are going to be free from the devil's decision, we must not only learn obedience, but we must learn to respond instantly and quickly to the Master's voice. Let's look at how obedience is the final key to reversing the devil's decision. But first, let's take a minute to review what we've discovered thus far.

We have studied what you need to reverse the devil's decision for your life:

- Endurance, the determination to keep going regardless of the circumstances

- Faith to believe God has something more for you than what you can feel or see

- Patience to wait for God's appointed time

You've endured, you've believed, you've waited and then God's appointed time to move finally arrives. What must you do to lay hold of the promise? You must obey. You must step out on the water.

THE WILL TO DO HIS WILL

I WANT TO begin by looking at two related passages of Scripture.

> Now about the midst of the feast Jesus went up into the temple, and taught. And the Jews marvelled, saying, How knoweth this man letters, having never learned? Jesus answered them, and said, My doctrine is not mine, but his that sent me. If any man will do his will, he shall know of the doctrine, whether it be of God, or whether I speak of myself.
> —JOHN 7:14–17, KJV

Jesus said, "If any man will do his will." We have to *will* to do His *will.*

Now the second passage:

> After this there was a feast of the Jews; and Jesus went up to Jerusalem. Now there is at Jerusalem by the sheep market a pool, which is called in the Hebrew tongue Bethesda, having five porches. In these lay a great multitude of impotent folk, of blind, halt, withered, waiting for the moving of the water. For an angel went down at a certain season

into the pool, and troubled the water: whosoever then first after the troubling of the water stepped in was made whole of whatsoever disease he had. And a certain man was there, which had an infirmity thirty and eight years. When Jesus saw him lie, and knew that he had been now a long time in that case, he saith unto him, Wilt thou be made whole? The impotent man answered him, Sir, I have no man, when the water is troubled, to put me into the pool: but while I am coming, another steppeth down before me. Jesus saith unto him, Rise, take up thy bed, and walk. And immediately the man was made whole, and took up his bed, and walked: and on the same day was the sabbath.

—JOHN 5:1–9, KJV

Jesus asked the man lying at the pool of Bethesda an interesting question: "Wilt thou be made whole?" In other words, is it *your* will to be made whole?

THE ANOINTING MAKES THE DIFFERENCE

DURING HIS EARTHLY ministry, Jesus ministered with a powerful anointing that distinguished Him from other men. When He was born He was just called Jesus. "And she will bring forth a Son, and you shall call His name JESUS, for He will save His people from their sins" (Matt. 1:21).

But from His baptism in the Jordan River—the inauguration point of His ministry—to being lifted up on the cross, He is referred to over and over again as either *Jesus Christ, Jesus the Christ* or simply *Christ.* The word *Christ* means "Messiah" or "Anointed One."

143

What gave Jesus distinction from other men was the power of the anointing of God upon His life.

What gave Jesus distinction from other men was the power of the anointing of God upon His life.

Outwardly, He appeared no different from other men. He didn't even look like a prophet. Isaiah described Him like this: "He has no form or comeliness; and when we see Him, there is no beauty that we should desire Him" (Isa. 53:2). Jesus was so ordinary looking that when the chief priests and elders came to arrest Him in the Garden of Gethsemane, they had to ask Judas Iscariot to point Him out.

Jesus' glory was not in the physical realm; it was in the realm of the supernatural. When Jesus the anointed Son of God spoke, demons trembled, people were healed and raging storms were stilled.

He walked through a cemetery and met a man who was possessed by demons. When Jesus commanded the demons to come out, they left screaming.

Jesus came upon a funeral procession as the people were carrying a young boy's body out of the village. He told them to stop, and then He spoke to the lifeless body lying in a coffin. The boy sat up and started speaking.

Jesus stood outside the tomb four days after Lazarus died and spoke, "Lazarus, come forth!" And out of that stinky tomb, still wrapped in grave clothes, came Lazarus.

THE ANOINTING MAKES YOU DIFFERENT

THE ANOINTING MADE a difference, but it also made Jesus different. He was not like all the other men. He didn't fit in with the religious clique of His day. One of the problems killing the church today is that we want to be in the clique with the good ol' boys.

Can you stand to be blessed? If you choose to be blessed, it won't be easy. You're going to be rejected when you're blessed. You have to be able to take a licking and keep on ticking. Not everybody is going to like you. But you have to make up your mind: Do you want to be popular or anointed?

> *Do you want to be popular or anointed?*

Jesus caused controversy everywhere He went. He disrupted the religious system when He threw the money-changers out of the temple courts. He called the Pharisees "whitewashed tombs." He astonished the people with His teaching because He taught as one who had divine authority—not like the scribes and teachers of the Law. The people loved Him, but the religious establishment hated Him.

The religious leaders wondered, *How in the world can He do what He is doing without going through our educational system? He's not learned; He hasn't been instructed. Who was His mentor?*

People always want to know where you came from. They always want to get in your business. They want to see if you have a right to minister. Instead of judging Jesus on the basis of healing people and setting them free, they just wanted to know about His credentials.

> And the Jews marvelled, saying, How knoweth this man letters, having never learned?
>
> —JOHN 7:15, KJV

And Jesus answered them, "My doctrine is not mine, but his that sent me" (John 7:16, KJV).

In other words, "I am not speaking of Myself; I speak of the power of God. I don't have My own agenda. I don't do My own thing. I do what God says. Not only am I speaking under the power and the anointing of God, but if any man desires to do God's will, he will know that the doctrine I speak is not Mine."

THE SOURCE OF REVELATION KNOWLEDGE

THE REASON THE religious leaders didn't know Jesus was sent from God was because their wills were not aligned with God's. Revelation knowledge, *rhema* knowledge, is imparted to us only as our wills are aligned with the will of God.

> *Revelation knowledge, rhema knowledge, is imparted to us only as our wills are aligned with the will of God.*

You can gather all your Bible facts and quote all the

scriptures you like, but as long as your will is out of line with the will of God, you'll have no revelation. You cannot educate it. You cannot intellectualize it. You have to pray your way into it. You have to lie before God and ask Him to give it to you in the name of Jesus.

Reversing the devil's decision isn't a matter of rational thinking; it comes as a result of revelation knowledge. The devil is sly and sinister. He'll whisper lies in your ear, and you'll think you're hearing truth. He'll twist Scripture to keep you in bondage to poverty, sickness and low self-esteem. But when you feed your spirit with the Word of God and your will comes into alignment with God's, God will impart to you His *rhema* knowledge. Suddenly you'll realize, "Jesus was wounded for *my* transgressions, He was bruised for *my* iniquities, the chastisement for *my* peace was upon Him, and by the stripes of Jesus Christ I AM HEALED!"

> *Reversing the devil's decision isn't a matter of rational thinking; it comes as a result of revelation knowledge.*

No one can teach you how to have a revelation. It is birthed as you cry out to God, "Lord, bring my will into alignment with Your own. Deliver me from being just one of the guys. Deliver me from being just one of the girls. Deliver me from being satisfied with just sitting on the missions board. I want to know You in the power of Your resurrection and the fellowship of Your sufferings."

THE RESPONSIBILITY OF HAVING A WILL

GOD DIDN'T HAVE to give us a will. In fact, it probably would have been much less of a hassle for Him if He hadn't! He could have made us computers or robots, but thank God He gave us a will. Because we have a will we can choose to love Him and we can enjoy the relationship that comes when two people choose to love each other.

But with a will also comes responsibility. God involves us in our own deliverance. And some of our deliverances require that we will to do His will to be successful.

God is not going to slap you in the face with deliverance. You're going to have to want to be delivered. God is not going to make you love another person. You're going to have to choose to love. God is not going to make you tear down racism and sexism. You're going to have to tear them down according to your own choice. God is not going to make you forgive. You are going to have to decide in your mind, *I will to do His will.*

Paul wrote in 1 Corinthians 14:15, "I *will* sing with the spirit, and I *will* also sing with the understanding (emphasis added). Paul decided to sing with the spirit and with the understanding.

Nobody is going to make you raise your hands in worship. Nobody is going to make you clap. Nobody is going to make you sing in the spirit or in the understanding. You have to will to do His will.

That's why Paul writes a little later in the same chapter, "The spirits of the prophets are subject to the prophets" (v. 32). This passage suggests that your spirit is subject to you. You have a will; God has a will. And God isn't going to put a gun to your head in order to make you align your will with His. You must will to do His will!

ALIGNING WITH GOD'S WILL ACTIVATES HIS POWER

AT THE POINT you bring your will into alignment, God will give you the grace for repentance, deliverance, forgiveness and change.

Aligning our will with God's activates His power. John wrote:

> Now this is the confidence that we have in Him, that if we ask anything according to His will, He hears us. And if we know that He hears us, whatever we ask, we know that we have the petitions that we have asked of Him.
>
> —1 JOHN 5:14–15

John was confident that when he willed to do God's will, God would answer his requests. Suddenly an entirely new supernatural world opened up before him. Can you see why it is so important for us to align our wills with God's? We *cannot* reverse the devil's decision without doing so first.

The night Jesus was betrayed He went to the Garden of Gethsemane and prayed that His will would be in alignment with the will of the Father. Three times He prayed until great drops of sweat fell like blood from His brow, and finally He declared, "Father, if it is Your will, take this cup away from Me; nevertheless *not My will, but Yours, be done*" (Luke 22:42, emphasis added).

EVERYBODY HAS THE WILL TO OVERCOME

IN HIS BACKSLIDDEN condition, even the prodigal son

living with the pigs in the muck and mire, with mud between his toes and corn husks in his hair, came to his senses. He said, "Wait a minute. I will arise and go." He said, "I will."

You have too much will in you to let the devil make the decisions for you. You have too much will to let him put his foot on you and hold you down. You have too much will to give up the fight. You just tell him, "I *will* get off drugs. I *will* stop abusing my wife. By the power of the Holy Ghost I *will* let go of my anger."

> *You have too much will in you to let the devil make the decisions for you.*

Don't let the devil's decision break your will. Don't let the struggles of life break your will. Don't let people, poverty, envy or guilt break your will. You need the will to reverse the devil's decision. You have to be able to say, "Though none assist me, none help me, none encourage me, none recognize me, none stand by me and none support me, nevertheless *I will.* Whatever it takes, *I will.*"

JUMPING WHEN GOD SAYS, "JUMP!"

JESUS WENT TO the pool of Bethesda where multitudes of sick people were lying. Tradition tells us that periodically an angel would stir the water, and the first one who got in the water after the angel touched it would be healed. The stirring of the water was a sign that the presence of God was there.

People ask, "When is it my time to be healed?" It is whenever the presence of Jesus is there. That is why the Bible says, "Today, if you will hear His voice, do not harden your hearts" (Heb. 3:15). God says, "Don't play hard to get with Me. You need to move when the water is stirred and My presence is there."

That's the way God moves, and that's the way we have to move. Suddenly, when God stirs the waters of opportunity in our lives, we have to jump in immediately. "Go get that job." "Go get that house." "Get ready. Here come the finances that I want you to bless others with." "Go write that book." "Go; now you can start that ministry." You have to do it when God says, "Go!" You can't wait for your friends. You can't wait to research it first before making the jump.

During such times of divine stirring, the most harmful thing a person can do is to fool around and miss his or her opportunity. The devil loves to divert our attention through envy, unbelief, anger and fear to cause us to miss our divinely appointed moment. We can be primed to follow God and have the endurance, faith and patience we need but still miss it because we got hung up on sin.

> *The most harmful thing a person can do is to fool around and miss his or her opportunity.*

REVERSE THE DEVIL'S DECISION

WHEN YOUR HEAD SAYS ONE THING
AND YOUR BODY SAYS ANOTHER

MANY SCHOLARS AGREE that the man lying by the pool of
Bethesda that day probably had cerebral palsy, a dis-
order that keeps the brain from communicating with the
rest of the body. A person with cerebral palsy can will to
pick up a glass, but the body won't fully cooperate.

The King James Version uses the word *impotent* to
describe the man. The term implies that his body was
lacking power or ability; it was unable to perform. This
man's brain gave commands to which his body did not
respond.

The man lying beside the pool of Bethesda was experiencing a rebellion—a mutiny—in his own body. When
the angel troubled the water, his head told his body to
get up, but instead of obeying, his body would fall
down. He willed to walk, but instead he sat. He
thought *move*, but his body lay motionless.

Isn't it terrible when you will to do one thing, but you
end up doing something else? Jesus said, "If a house be
divided against itself, that house cannot stand" (Mark
3:25, KJV).

Your physical house is divided against itself when
you're trying to get up, but you can't get up. You're
trying to be free, but you can't be free. You're trying to
be delivered, but you can't be delivered.

This man experienced thirty-eight years of frustration
trying to get into the pool in time. Others have been
impotent in different ways. Some have experienced
thirty-eight years of trying to build a marriage that
wouldn't work or thirty-eight years working a dead-end

job or thirty-eight years not speaking to your mother or thirty-eight years of being at war with your daughter.

Have you experienced thirty-eight years of feeling trapped in the devil's decision and you don't know how to get out? Every time you have tried you have fallen flat on your face. You don't want to live like this. You don't want to treat people like this. You keep telling yourself you're going to do better, but you don't.

If you live in bondage long enough, eventually you tell yourself, "Well, maybe I wasn't meant to get up." You make a home out of what should have been just a temporary circumstance. The pool of Bethesda becomes familiar territory. You decide, "I guess things aren't going to get any better for me. I guess I'll never be free. I guess I'll just accept the devil's decision for my poverty, sickness, joblessness, welfare. Even though I'll never be happy, maybe my children will be happy." But just when you resign yourself to lying there beside your own pool of Bethesda, here comes Jesus!

WILT THOU?

THE MAN HAD been at the pool for thirty-eight years, and Jesus asked him the most ridiculous question, "Do you want to be made well?" (John 5:6).

He must have thought, *Do I want to be well? Do you think that I am here because I want to be here?*

Don't you understand that every time it looked as if my deliverance had come, and the angel was stirring the waters, I would get up only to fall down? And while I was trying to get myself together so I could get in the pool, somebody would get there before me. I didn't have a chance. But I just kept trying to get up.

No! It's not my will to be like this. I'm not like this because I didn't want to get to the pool. It's just that my command center wasn't working with my flesh.

Paul wrote, "For the good that I will to do, I do not do; but the evil I will not to do, that I practice" (Rom. 7:19). When you will to do the right thing, but everywhere you go, evil is present, how do you break free from the devil's decision for your life?

BREAKING FREE

THE MAN LYING at the pool didn't think his time had come. The waters weren't stirring, and he didn't even have someone to help him get in the pool. That is, until Jesus showed up. Wherever Jesus is, Satan's power is broken. Whenever you align your will with Jesus' will, you have the ingredients for an unscheduled miracle!

> *Whenever you align your will with Jesus' will, you have the ingredients for an unscheduled miracle!*

It doesn't matter if it isn't the right time or the right day or the right place. Just when you decide that nothing good is going to happen, God opens the windows of heaven and pours a blessing into your lap that you can't even contain. Just when the devil has decided that your life is over, the Holy Ghost speaks up and says, "The devil's a liar!" Just when you're about to throw in the towel and quit, God says, "I'm going to resurrect you."

Jesus said, "Do you want to be made well?"

"Of course I do. It's not my will to be like this."

Then Jesus said, "Rise, take up your bed and walk" (John 5:8).

"Jesus, didn't You hear what I said? I don't have anyone to help me get into the pool, and I can't do it by myself. In addition to not being able to control my own body, You want me to pick up this bed? Lord, I can't pick up the bed because I'm *in* the bed. How can I pick up what I am lying in?"

But when this impotent man at the pool of Bethesda aligned his will with God's and decided to obey, he was instantly freed from his bed of bondage.

When you will to do the will of Jesus, God gives you the power to take hold of the thing that has taken hold of you and the grace to carry the things that used to carry you. If poverty has you crippled, if habitual sin has you bedfast, if a low self-image has you paralyzed, God can give you the power to rise out of that bed and walk.

> *When you will to do the will of Jesus, God gives you the power to take hold of the thing that has taken hold of you.*

When you align your will with God's and choose to reverse the devil's decision for your life, your bed becomes your testimony. You're not ashamed of the bed that you carry in your hands because it no longer has you. You show it off to everybody and tell them how they can be delivered from their beds, too!

Now that's a complete reversal of the devil's decision!

SECTION III
WINNING THE VICTORY

Chapter 12

Beating Panic and Fear

W HEN YOU FACE an unexpected storm, when the enemy comes in like a flood, what is your normal reaction? Do you panic? Are you overwhelmed? Do you sit and stare in disbelief, blinking like a frog in a hailstorm? Although no one would choose to weather a storm, it's the storm that reveals what you're made of.

In this section we are going to look at how you can reverse the various decisions the devil makes for your life to prevent you from living the abundant life Jesus promises every believer.

I believe that the Word works. Staying in the Word of God will keep you from going crazy and doing foolish things that will take you years to recover from. You can relax in Christ when other people are sinking because you have the peaceful assurance that your foundation is stable and sure.

Jesus said in Matthew 7:21:

> Not everyone who says to Me, "Lord, Lord," shall
> enter the kingdom of heaven, but he who does
> the will of My Father in heaven.

A lot of folks talk about the Lord, but that doesn't
mean they're going to experience the benefits or blessings that come from knowing the Lord in their daily
lives. Jesus continued His explanation:

> Many will say to Me in that day, "Lord, Lord,
> have we not prophesied in Your name, cast out
> demons in Your name, and done many wonders
> in Your name?" And then I will declare to them,
> "I never knew you; depart from Me, you who
> practice lawlessness!"
>
> Therefore whoever hears these sayings of
> Mine, and does them, I will liken him to a wise
> man who built his house on the rock: and the rain
> descended, the floods came, and the winds blew
> and beat on that house; and it did not fall, for it
> was founded on the rock. But everyone who
> hears these sayings of Mine, and does not do
> them, will be like a foolish man who built his
> house on the sand: and the rain descended, the
> floods came, and the winds blew and beat on that
> house; and it fell. And great was its fall.
>
> —MATTHEW 7:22–27

OVERCOMING PANIC WITH THE WORD

ONE OF THE devil's decisions for your life is to get you to
panic and to begin bouncing around emotionally, this

way and that, like a rubber ball. He wants you so confused and mixed up that you don't know who you are or how to handle the situation you're in.

I get excited reading this text because it tells me what the Word of God is able to do for me. The Word can preach power into me. I've been sick, and the Word of God has preached sickness out of my body. I've been discouraged, and it preached discouragement out of my mind. I have suffered from panic attacks, and the Word of God preached the panic attacks out of my life.

That's why it's important to get to a church that preaches the Word. Staying home and reading your Bible is not enough. You need to hear the Word preached so you can get it into your spirit. Then you will find out that the Word of God really does work.

But many people who go to church aren't worshiping the Lord; they're just being religious. In some cities and towns it's fashionable to go to church, particularly to attend certain kinds of churches that pride themselves on the who's who lists of names that attend. Some individuals go to a certain church because it helps them to climb up their professional ladder.

More important than attending the "right" church is having a genuine experience with Jesus Christ. You have to know beyond a shadow of a doubt that Jesus is the Lord of your life. Never go to church for religious reasons. When you walk into church, always be sure you can say, "I'm here because Jesus Christ is the most important thing in my life."

There is a difference between a casual, superficial experience with God and a personal relationship with the King of kings and Lord of lords. Seek the kind of relationship that imparts to you the power and anointing of Jesus Christ so you can face a storm without panic.

But you need to understand, it's not a matter of being in the "right" church; it's being in a church where you hear the Word preached and where you develop a relationship with the living Word, Jesus Christ.

Jesus blatantly stated that not everyone who says "Lord, Lord" is going to enter into the kingdom of heaven. Not everybody who says "Thank God" really knows God. Not everybody who says "Hallelujah" really has praise on his or her lips. In the last days Jesus said some will say, "Lord, we've done great works in Your name. We've healed the sick. We raised the dead. We gave money. We did this. We did that."

But Jesus will declare, "I never knew you; depart from Me, you who practice lawlessness!" (Matt. 7:23). In other words, the Lord will say, "You did the right thing, but you did it for the wrong reason." These individuals had the head knowledge; they may have even attended the right church, but they never built the foundation of their lives on a personal relationship with Jesus Christ.

PANIC RESULTS FROM BEING BUILT ON THE WRONG FOUNDATION

THE REASON PANIC, turmoil and anxiety become so strong in people's lives is because the foundation they are built on is faulty. Their faulty foundations cannot hold them up in times of difficulty or trouble. Having the right foundation is imperative because without it, you will never be able to withstand the storms of life.

Your foundation as an individual as well as your family's foundation remains hidden beyond what the human eye can see. How foolish it is to invest in a beautiful house when the foundation of your home is faulty. Even more foolish is to invest your whole life into what others can see while at the same time neglecting the far more important qualities that cannot be seen.

The greatest investment you can make is not investing in the image you project or in being overly concerned in what people think. For you will quickly discover that peoples' opinions about you will change every day. One day you will be a hero, and the next day you'll be a dog. One day you'll be wonderful; the next day no one will even talk to you.

> *The greatest investment you can make is not investing in the image you project or in being overly concerned in what people think.*

The greatest investment you can make is investing into the person you really are—the person others rarely see. Investing into your own godly character creates the foundation that lies below the surface: beneath your makeup or your tie, beyond the car or the house. Jesus was saying that it's not the outward things that will help you to make it through times of trouble. What you need is a solid foundation.

THE CORNERSTONE
MAKES THE DIFFERENCE

WHEN GOD GOT ready to build the church of Jesus Christ, He wasn't worried about the structure or the

163

appearance. But He was very concerned about the chief cornerstone. He knew if He could lay the right cornerstone in the right place, then it wouldn't matter what kind of storm came against the house. It would be able to withstand anything.

In Matthew 16, Jesus asked His disciples who they thought He was. Did they consider Him a prophet or something more than a prophet? Peter answered, "You are the Christ, the Son of the living God." Jesus answered, "On this rock"—Peter's confession of Christ—"I will build My church, and the gates of Hades shall not prevail against it" (Matt. 16:13–18).

What matters most about your life is the cornerstone that it is built upon. If Jesus, the living Word, is your cornerstone, then all the powers of hell can come against you and you'll be able to withstand all of them. You will declare, "No weapon formed against me—sickness, disease, poverty or lack—shall prosper or hinder me from moving forward. I may be blown around; I may get bent over. I may have blood running out of the corner of my mouth and dust on my face. But don't write me off. Don't tell me I'll never make it, because my foundation is secure. I don't have to panic or get overwhelmed by fear because God's Word says, 'I know whom I have believed and am persuaded that He is able to keep what I have committed to Him until that Day'" (2 Tim. 1:12).

Jesus—the living Word—is the cornerstone of our lives. But we also need something to complete the building of our foundation, something that will not move or change. We need the Word of God.

THE DIFFERENCE BETWEEN THE TWO MEN

JESUS TOLD THE story of two men. The first man built his house on the rock, and when the storms hit and the floods came and the winds blew, his house stood firm. The second man, however, wanted to build his house on oceanfront property because he liked the view. But when he built it, he didn't consider what might happen to his house since its foundation was on the sand. Once the storms hit and the floods came and the winds blew, his house collapsed. In fact, the Bible tells us "it fell with a great crash" (Matt. 7:27, NIV).

The two men in Jesus' story had one thing in common: They both heard the Word. Jesus said that whoever heard His sayings and did them is like one of the two men (Matt. 7:24). One man heard the Word and *didn't* do it. The other man heard the Word *and did it.*

Now hearing the Word is a wonderful thing. Christians are getting more Word now than ever. Through the airwaves you can watch Christian television and listen to Christian radio. You can walk into a Bible bookstore and pick up any number of books that teach the Word. We have more translations of the Bible than anyone can count. Every day, it seems we have greater access to the Word.

The very fact that you're reading this book is evidence that you and I believe something happens when we're exposed to the Word. When we are exposed to the Word, it can get down inside of us and begin building a foundation of faith.

Some people say, "Well that's good. That will make the difference." Well no, hearing the Word will not

165

bring victory into your life. Hearing the Word is important. But there's a difference between *hearing* the Word and *doing* the Word.

> *Hearing the Word is important. But there's a difference between hearing the Word and doing the Word.*

Plenty of folks have heard the Word, but they're not doing anything about it. And because they haven't acted on it, they've grown lazy and fat. That's why you can look at some people and wonder, "How did that person get panicked and become so crazy? They've been coming here to church for years."

Some of the most miserable, defeated, fickle, moody people I know are sitting in churches every week.

Now please pay close attention to this point: The man who heard the Word and *didn't* do it constructed as nice of a house as the man who heard the Word and *did* it. If you drove by, you wouldn't have been able to tell any difference. As you drove by, you'd say, "Oh, wow! Both houses are nice! The guy who *didn't* do anything has just as nice of a house as the guy who *did* do something."

Now faith doesn't come by doing it. Faith comes just by hearing it. "Faith comes by hearing, and hearing by the word of God" (Rom. 10:17). That's why I tell people, "Don't stop coming to church. You may have messed up. You might be as wrong as three left shoes, but just keep coming. There's still hope for you. You may be in a turmoil and crisis, but if you can just stay under the preaching and teaching of the Word, there's still some hope for you."

THE STORM TELLS ALL

THERE ARE FOLKS getting full of the Word. They listen to teaching tapes; the men go to men's meetings, and the women go to women's meetings. They listen to an anointed man or woman who is ministering at a nearby church. But when they come back, the women are still gossiping and complaining and the men are still mistreating their wives. What seems to be the problem?

Now, not everybody is like that. Some people are changed through the tapes and meetings and seminars. But a lot of people hear the Word, yet it does them no good.

The man in the parable looked as if he were doing just fine by hearing the Word. He had built a beautiful house, and if you drove by, you couldn't tell it was different from any other house.

If you've built your life on sand, you will feel like everyone else. Until the doctor says, "Your blood count is different than it was last month." Until a police officer knocks on your door and tells you, "We've arrested your daughter on drug charges." Until you go to work on Monday morning and learn that your job has been terminated.

Everything looks the same until a storm comes your way. Before the storm comes, you don't have to worry about dealing with the panic. Before the storm, you can't tell the saint from the sinner. You can't tell who's real and who's playing. You can't tell who's sincere or who's just putting on a front.

> *Before the storm, you can't tell the saint from the sinner.*

But when the storm comes, it very quickly becomes easy to separate the sheep from the goats. During the storm you can tell who is playing church and who knows what church is really all about. You'll identify the folks who have had a superficial, carnal experience and those who really know who they are in Christ.

It's the storm that helps you to understand what caliber of a person you're dealing with. It's the storm that reveals who you really are.

When the day of evil comes, will you be able to stand? When you come face to face with the devil's decision, will you have the presence of mind to reverse it? Will you have peace and strength through the power and the might of the Holy Ghost, or will you go crazy because of the storm? If your life isn't built on something that is solid, stable and secure, there are storms out there that can blow your mind.

When the storm hit, the Bible says the rain fell, the floods came and the wind blew against the house. The storm beat against everything the man had built: his career, relationships and reputation. When a storm comes, it beats against everything you have ever built.

During a storm, people who have said, "I'll stay with you," will walk away and leave you. A real storm can send a rich man into financial chaos. A real storm can leave a healthy man feeling sick. You may have a marriage like Ozzie and Harriet's, but in a real storm you can stop speaking to each another for months. A real storm can come against everything around you to break you down.

That's why you need a foundation in the Word of God that is sure and stable, so you will know how to act, so you will know how to talk, so you will know how to walk and so you will know how to handle yourself when the storm comes.

And the Bible says that when the storm beat against the house built on the sand, great was its fall.

SAME HOUSE, SAME STORM, DIFFERENT FOUNDATION

THE SAME PARABLE tells us about another man. This man built the same house as the first man; it had just as many doors, just as many windows, just as much brick, just as many rooms and just as fine a roof.

This other man also faced the same storm. It doesn't matter how holy your life is or how much you obey the Word, you may face storms in your life that are just as fierce as the storms that come against the unrighteous. But you don't have to get panicky. You won't quit God and quit church as long as you know that your hope is built on nothing less than Jesus' blood and righteousness.

> *It doesn't matter how holy your life is or how much you obey the Word, you may face storms in your life that are just as fierce as the storms that come against the unrighteous.*

The difference between the two men in the parable was this: One chose to act on the Word, and the other didn't. Both were faithful church attenders who tithed every week and sang in the choir. But when the storm came, only one stood against the devil and said, "Devil, I will not be moved because the Bible says I am more than a conqueror. I come against you by the word of my testimony and the blood of the Lamb. As long as I'm on the solid foundation, you can't move me and you can't break me. You might shake me a little, but when this storm is over, I'll be standing taller than when it started. The shutters on my windows may blow off, my gutters may sag and my roof may even leak once in a while, but I'm built on the Rock. On Christ the solid Rock I stand; all other ground is sinking sand!"

You may be going through the same storm that the ungodly folks are going through, but that's all right because you know something that they don't know. Their hope is built on their money. It's built on their career. It's built upon who they are in the community. It's built upon their talent. But if you belong to the Lord Jesus, your life is built on the chief cornerstone. When Jesus is the corner of your foundation, no matter what comes against you—sickness, disease, lack or any other decision the devil has made for your life—it *cannot* prevail. You can't help but stand firm because Jesus is the chief cornerstone.

A fierce storm can be pretty scary. It's easy to get panicky. You might even be tempted to run away. But if you leave the house, the storm may kill you. Sometimes to reverse the devil's decision, you have to stand. Your heart may fill with fear. If it does, keep standing against it afraid. Keep speaking the Word of God that has formed a powerful foundation within you.

If you struggle with panic and fear, you need to follow Paul's advice:

> Finally, brethren, whatever things are true, whatever things are noble, whatever things are just, whatever things are pure, whatever things are lovely, whatever things are of good report, if there is any virtue and if there is anything praiseworthy—meditate on these things.
>
> —PHILIPPIANS 4:8

You don't get rid of negative, panicky thoughts by trying *not* to think about them; you overcome them by continually choosing the truth until the negative thoughts are overwhelmed by the power of the truth.

THE STORM IS A MATTER OF PERSPECTIVE

DO YOU REMEMBER when you were a child trying to sleep through a storm at night? Every time the thunder crashed or a tree branch tapped against your window, you knew the world was coming to an end. If you dared to look out the window, you were sure you could see the boogey man trying to break into your house. But as an adult, watching a storm can be exciting because it displays the awesome power of God.

In the same way, when the storm hits, you can hear the crashing and make the choice to believe that your world is coming to an end, or you can sit back and enjoy watching an awesome display of the power of God.

When the children of Israel were trapped between the Red Sea and the oncoming Egyptian army—a storm if there ever was one—God spoke:

Fear not; stand still (firm, confident, undismayed) and see the salvation of the Lord which He will work for you today.

—EXODUS 14:13, AMP

The devil hides in the shadows. He dwells in the realm of imaginations. He feeds on fear. And to act on that fear—to panic—is to act as if Satan is bigger than God. But once we realize that our fear is

F—alse
E—vidence
A—ppearing
R—eal,

we understand that what we are afraid of may not even exist at all. But even if it *is* real, our God is bigger. Because Jesus defeated death and the grave, no power on earth is stronger.

The greatest battles being fought today are not on the battlefield of foreign wars; they're fought in the minds of men and women. The battle *you* fight against panic will take place in *your* mind. You must be consistent—you must continually feed on the Word. You must believe it and act on it.

At the same time, you can't expect to hear the Word and not obey it and then when the storm hits, to successfully stand against it. You can prepare to overcome panic by acting NOW! Obey the Word NOW! Do what it says NOW! Then when the storms come, your foundation will be strong and the power of God's Word will strengthen you to stand firm until the storm has passed and all is peaceful once more.

Chapter 13

Deliverance From Discouragement and Hopelessness

THE DEVIL WAS holding a yard sale one day and displayed his most useful tools, marked at different prices, on a table. Lying side by side were some of his most notable implements of destruction: hatred, envy, jealousy, deceit, lust, lying and pride—all on sale. But over to the side of the yard on display was a worn-out tool that cost more than all the others combined. The tool was labeled DISCOURAGEMENT.

When asked why it was more expensive than the other tools, the devil responded, "It's more useful to me than any of the others. When I can't bring down my victims with the rest of my tools, I use discouragement, because so few people realize it belongs to me."[1]

Nothing paralyzes us, nothing stops us in our tracks like discouragement and its partner in crime, hopelessness. Discouragement and hopelessness are no respecters of persons. They keep the unemployed unemployed. The homeless homeless. The sick sick. They can even draw the most powerful ministry to its knees.

When you're overcome with discouragement and hopelessness, you can't pray, you can't worship and you become a victim of your environment. Discouragement and hopelessness drain you of courage, vision, faith, expectation and the will to make a difference in the kingdom of God. If the devil can get you discouraged and hopeless, then he has successfully neutralized you. You are left with only enough energy to feel sorry for yourself.

> *If the devil can get you discouraged and hopeless, then he has successfully neutralized you.*

DISCOURAGEMENT'S DOWNWARD SPIRAL

WHEN CIRCUMSTANCES DON'T go according to plan, you are disappointed. You're sorry things didn't work out, but your life goes on.

When you allow those circumstances to affect your feelings and to influence your behavior, you become discouraged. The word *discourage* literally means "to deprive of courage," so you lack the courage to try again or even continue as you did before.

Over time, discouragement turns into hopelessness because you lose any hope or expectation that your disappointing circumstances will ever change.

The final stage in this downward spiral is depression.

When you're depressed, you can do little more than eat and sleep.

What begins as disappointment becomes discouragement, turns into hopelessness and ends up as depression. The longer a person continues in this progression, the harder it is to be delivered from it.

Reversing the devil's decision in this area is difficult because the person suffering from this emotional trauma rarely cares. Every day grows darker, gloomier and more hopeless. You cry out, "God, are You even there? Do You care?" And so often the pain you feel drowns out God's loving reply, "Yes."

THE FIVEFOLD CAUSES OF DISCOURAGEMENT

IT IS IMPORTANT to understand the relationship between feelings and circumstances. When you tie your emotions to your situation, you set yourself up for discouragement. There are five causes of discouragement.

> *Any time you tie your emotions to your situation, you set yourself up for discouragement.*

1. Exaggeration of your circumstances

Moses sent twelve men into Canaan to spy out the Promised Land. When they returned, the reports between Caleb and Joshua and the other ten were completely different. While Caleb and Joshua were looking at the grapes, the other ten men were looking at the giants. God had delivered the children of Israel from slavery in Egypt.

He had parted the Red Sea, fed them manna and given them water to drink out of a rock, yet the ten men—and the rest of Israel—couldn't believe God was bigger than the giants in the land.

The devil loves to blow our circumstances out of proportion. We grow discouraged when we start looking at what the situation dictates instead of what God says in His Word.

2. Exhaustion

You may find this hard to believe, but many ministers struggle with discouragement after being used of God. You can minister in the power of the Holy Ghost, see God use you to touch lives in a mighty way and go home and fight discouragement. By the end of the day, you're mentally, physically, emotionally and spiritually exhausted. That's when the devil sneaks into your room and tells you, *God wasn't using you. You were making it all up. Everything you saw today was nothing but emotion. The people you thought were delivered weren't delivered. They'll go right back to the same bondage. You're nothing but a useless windbag.*

Sometimes one of the best things you can do to fight discouragement is to slow down and get some rest because when you're tired, you can't pray. When you're tired, you can't hear the voice of God. When you're tired, you don't have the strength to reverse the devil's decision for your life.

3. Dashed expectations

Some people may call them disappointments, but they may only be detours. A detour is simply another route that takes you to the same destination.

You start dating the person you're sure you're going to marry. All of a sudden the other person breaks off the engagement, and you feel as if your life is ruined! You're on a detour. How do you know God doesn't have someone better for you?

You start a career in a certain field, and you experience a detour. Some people call it unemployment, but how do you know God isn't leading you into a far more rewarding and prosperous occupation? When you're on a detour, don't get discouraged and down and mad at God! He may be leading you into something better than what you already have.

How often do we make plans for our lives without considering that God's plans for our lives may be different? But if I had to choose between God's plans and my plans, I'd choose God's in a heartbeat. Here is a glimpse of God's plans for your life:

> "For I know the plans I have for you," declares
> the LORD, "plans to prosper you and not to harm
> you, plans to give you hope and a future."
> —JEREMIAH 29:11, NIV

God's plans always bring hope—never discouragement or dashed expectations. If anything, God's expectations for your life far surpass your own!

God's plans always bring hope—never discouragement or dashed expectations. If anything, God's expectations for your life far surpass your own!

---

4. Guilt

Guilt is the feeling of remorse and responsibility for a sin that has been committed. We feel remorseful when the Holy Ghost convicts us of a particular sin. At that point we can choose to continue in remorse or take responsibility for our sins and bring them to the cross of Jesus for forgiveness.

One subtle way the enemy uses his tool of discouragement is by continually bringing us back to the sins we have already been forgiven of. Often we keep coming back to God, praying, "Dear God, I'm sorry for that sin I committed ten years ago." But God says, "I have no idea what you're talking about because that's all under the blood of Jesus."

If you have unconfessed sin, make it right with God and move on with your life. But if you keep getting overwhelming feelings of guilt and condemnation, then you need to tell the devil, "I may not be perfect, but the blood of Jesus has cleansed me of every stain. Because of that, in God's eyes I *am* perfect! 'There is therefore now no condemnation to those who are in Christ Jesus'" (Rom. 8:1).

5. True disappointment

Perhaps you married that man after all, and he became abusive, or you married that woman, and she began cheating on you behind your back. Perhaps you were laid off from your job, and you couldn't find another one. The result is true disappointment.

On the other hand, you may be truly disappointed in yourself because you keep falling back into your old sinful habits. And because you can't seem to shake loose of those besetting sins, you feel discouraged, hopeless and maybe even depressed. You ask yourself, *Why would God ever want to rescue me? I might as well give up!*

A WORD OF HOPE

THE DEVIL WANTS you to feel hopeless in your situation. He tells you, "Things are never going to be different. You're never going to change. You'll never get your act together, so you might as well give up."

Well, I have one thing to say about that: The devil is a liar!

You need to know the Word so you can know what God says. And anything that comes to your mind that's opposite of what God's Word says is because God's not saying it! If God's not saying it, then the devil must be saying it, and because the devil is a liar, it must not be true.

Regardless of the cause of your disappointment, discouragement, hopelessness or even depression, there is a word that can give you the hope and the courage to reverse the devil's decision for your life. I hope you never forget this word:

SUDDENLY!!!

Disappointments, troubles and circumstances can and do drastically change SUDDENLY! I want to wake up every day with the expectancy that there is no telling what God may SUDDENLY do today!

GOOD THINGS COME TO THOSE WHO WAIT

And being assembled together with them, He [Jesus] commanded them not to depart from Jerusalem, but to wait for the Promise of the

179

Father, "which," He said, "you have heard from
Me."

—ACTS 1:4

After Jesus had risen from the dead, He met with His
disciples a few more times to give them parting instructions before ascending to His Father. But first, He
commanded them to wait. It wasn't a suggestion.

Waiting on God is not some passive, apathetic, lazy,
fatalistic mode wherein you just sit back and do nothing.
Waiting means you only do what God tells you to do,
what God anoints you to do and what God gives you
permission to do. And when you've done that—even if it
takes six months or six years—then you don't do anything else until God tells you to do something else.

> *Waiting means you only do what God tells you to
> do, what God anoints you to do and what God
> gives you permission to do.*

WAITING ON GOD MEANS NOT MOVING AHEAD

WAITING INVOLVES TWO realms: The first is *the outer
realm.* It means *not* going out in the flesh and trying to
make something happen. We don't move ahead of God
or apart from God because the flesh profits nothing.
(See John 6:63.) In other words, it will only set us back
to where we end up working against God's plan.

To the nonbeliever as well as the Christian who isn't
spiritually discerning, waiting seems to be a waste of
time. "What are you doing sitting around? Do you think

anything's going to happen with you just sitting there? You need to grab the bull by the horns and take control of your situation!"

But God has a method. Something very important must happen before God can move in our situations: We have to run completely out of ourselves. We have to get to the place where we know that in our own strength we cannot accomplish whatever it is that needs to be done, and if we tried, we'd fail or foul it up.

God commanded the disciples to wait for the promise of the Holy Spirit. He said, "Don't you try to perform any mighty acts in My name until you have received the promise of the Holy Spirit. If you do go out beforehand, you'll only make fools of yourselves and fall flat on your faces."

Just because you are baptized in the Holy Spirit doesn't mean you can assume that God is anointing everything you do. When you wait on God, refusing to move ahead without His guiding you, the anointing is released because it honors God. You can't take the credit for your success because you didn't make it happen. God did!

> *Just because you are baptized in the Holy Spirit doesn't mean you can assume that God is anointing everything you do.*

WAITING ON GOD IS PRAYERFUL

THE SECOND REALM that waiting involves is *the inner realm*. We need to keep our emotions, our thoughts and our wills at peace while we look in expectation for

God to lead us forward. Although we may not appear to be doing anything at all, waiting is really an act of faith! The one thing we *can* do is pray.

> **Although we may not appear to be doing anything at all, waiting is really an act of faith!**

The temptation we face in the outer realm is the same temptation we face in the inner realm: We want control. In the outer realm we move ahead of God and end up messing everything up. In the inner realm, we barge into prayer and start talking ninety miles a minute without any thought of what God wants.

If you're having a fit every ten minutes, peeking at your watch and looking around the room to see if anything is happening, you're not waiting. You're still full of yourself. You're still anxious, and you're trying to make something happen in the flesh.

Instead, you need to go into prayer and humble yourself. You need to say, "God, I don't know what to say. So I'm going to wait on You."

WHAT HAPPENS WHEN YOU FAIL TO WAIT

JUST WAITING ON God releases the anointing that enables you to do what you ought to do. But whenever you violate either realm—the inner realm or the outer realm—you haven't honored God by waiting on Him, and you end up acting in the flesh.

Sometimes you have something to say to someone that *really* needs to be said. Maybe it's a sin issue that needs to be confronted. But if you run into the situation blabbing your mouth and moving ahead of God or His timing, you'll just make a big mess. It might be a good idea, but it's not going to work if you don't wait on God.

When God formed Adam out of the dust of the earth, the framework was there, but something was missing. Adam needed God to breathe into him the breath of life.

No matter how good an idea you have, if you don't wait on God to breathe His breath of life into it, it's not going to get up on its feet and live.

> *No matter how good an idea you have, if you don't wait on God to breathe His breath of life into it, it's not going to get up on its feet and live.*

WAITING TO RECEIVE POWER

JESUS INSTRUCTED HIS disciples to wait until they received power from on high. Jesus was laying down a life principle for the New Testament church: You need to wait until the anointing is there to lead you ahead.

You can get Ishmael any time you want him, but if you want Isaac, you have to wait. You see, Ishmael was the child of Abraham produced by the flesh, but Isaac was the child of promise and faith. (See Genesis 16.)

> *You can get Ishmael any time you want him, but if*
> *you want Isaac, you have to wait.*

So they waited. Here's how Acts 1:13 in the Amplified Version describes it: "And when they had entered [the city], they mounted [the stairs] to the upper room where they were [*indefinitely*] staying" (emphasis added).

The disciples decided to stay indefinitely. They had the mind-set, "We're going to that upper room for the long haul and we're not coming out of there until God shows up! It doesn't matter if it takes ten minutes or ten months; we're waiting until God leads us out of there!"

Right there is our problem. In the church today we have had so much zeal in our flesh that even if we get around to waiting on God, we only do it for short periods of time before our flesh takes over again. If God doesn't do something when we want Him to do it, or as quickly as we want Him to do it, then our bright ideas overtake us, and we get right back into the flesh.

REVERSING THE DEVIL'S
DECISION FOR DISCOURAGEMENT

YOU NEED THE same mind-set when dealing with discouragement, hopelessness and depression. When this is your mind-set, you say, "I've come to the end of myself. I've tried to handle it on my own, but it's obvious I can't pull this off. My deliverance MUST come from You, God. I'm going to wait on You until You lead me out."

So many people have been healed—whether emotionally, spiritually or physically—while they waited in the presence of God. They realized they couldn't do it on their own, so they just spent time in His presence. Maybe they wept. Maybe they read the Word. Maybe they acted like a little child and cried, "God! I can't help myself! If You don't change me, I'll stay this way until the trumpet blows!"

How long do you need to wait on God? Indefinitely. That's the key word. You have to come to the point where you're going to wait indefinitely.

> *How long do you need to wait on God? Indefinitely.*

One hundred twenty of Jesus' followers gathered in the upper room to wait indefinitely for the promise of the Holy Spirit. Jesus had spent three years preparing them to continue His work. Everything was ready in heaven, but they still needed to wait on God for ten more days. They didn't try to make something happen. They waited on God to do it.

They weren't being passive; they were waiting with patience and confident expectancy. They knew God could suddenly show up at any minute and change the entire situation in an instant.

SUDDENLY!

> When the Day of Pentecost had fully come, they
> were all with one accord in one place. *And sud-*
> *denly* there came a sound from heaven, as of a
> rushing mighty wind, and it filled the whole
> house where they were sitting.
>
> —ACTS 2:1–2, EMPHASIS ADDED

The people in the upper room had no idea when
God would show up or what would happen when He
did. But He showed up and poured out His Holy Spirit
just as He had promised.

And that's the way God wants to move in our lives.

When you've waited and waited and your circumstances still haven't changed. When you feel that you
can't stand it one more second, but you're still holding
on, trusting God with simple faith.

Then SUDDENLY God moves in your life. He often
moves when you least expect it. God never appears the
way you think. You might be looking out the front door,
and He comes in the back door.

That's why we need to stop trying to figure out what
God is going to do. One of the greatest burdens you can
take on is the burden of trying to figure God out. "*How* is
God going do it? *When* is He going to do it? When, God,
when?"

Jesus answered that question in Acts 1:6–7:

> Therefore, when they had come together, they
> asked Him, saying, "Lord, will You at this time
> restore the kingdom to Israel?" And He said to
> them, "It is not for you to know times or seasons
> which the Father has put in His own authority."

The disciples wanted to know when Jesus was going to return, and He answered them, "It is not for you to know the times or seasons." Our responsibility is to wait on God. The responsibility for the timing of His visitation belongs to Him.

> *Our responsibility is to wait on God. The responsibility for the timing of His visitation belongs to Him.*

THERE'S A SUDDENLY IN YOUR LIFE, TOO

IN ACTS 16, Paul and Silas were sitting in a jail cell at midnight. Their hands and feet were in stocks. They had been beaten with rods, and now they were bloody and grimy. But they were singing songs, and the other prisoners were listening to them.

SUDDENLY there was an earthquake. The shackles fell off the prisoners' arms and legs, the prison doors swung wide open and the captives were set free!

God broke into the middle of their horrible circumstances because circumstances cannot stand for one second before the power of God. That's how great our God is!

> *Circumstances cannot stand for one second before the power of God. That's how great our God is!*

But you can't defeat your circumstances without God's help. If you start messing with your circumstances, they may only get worse. In fact, I think we exalt our circumstances to a place that's far too high by paying too much attention to them.

Discouragement sets in when we do everything we know to do and it still doesn't work. That's why we're better off letting God worry about circumstances.

If you or somebody you know is struggling with discouragement, hopelessness or depression, know this: All at once, SUDDENLY everything can change. Your job situation can turn around. Your son or daughter can get saved. Any decision the devil has made for your life or the life of a loved one can be reversed.

Rather than frustrating yourself further by trying to change your circumstances, the best thing you can do is wait on God. Spend time in God's presence. Humble yourself before Him and acknowledge to Him that He is the only One who can change your situation. The Bible says, "Therefore humble yourselves under the mighty hand of God, that He may exalt you in due time, casting all your care upon Him, for He cares for you" (1 Pet. 5:6–7).

When we get out of God's way, we give Him room to do great things and reverse the devil's decision for discouragement and hopelessness in our lives.

Chapter 14

Like a
Junkyard Dog

I F YOU HAVEN'T already, chances are that in your lifetime you will run into some mean-spirited folk—
people who treat you meaner than a junkyard dog. They
are people who will blow through your life and leave
you in a heap of rejection and hurt that you hardly know
what to do with. The saddest fact is that you may run
into these people at church. So when the devil decides
to wound you, you need to know how to reverse his
decision and win the victory. Let's take a look at David,
a man after God's own heart.

David was God's man. He didn't always look like
God's man: He didn't have the look of a person who
was going to be successful, and he certainly didn't look
like he was marked to be king. But he was.

There was one obstacle standing in the way of David
becoming king. He was an outsider. Not only was he

not in line to inherit the throne, but he wasn't even related to the king. He was also an outsider in his own home.

But after Saul had disqualified himself in God's eyes to serve as the king of Israel, God instructed the prophet Samuel to anoint another king. He led Samuel to the home of Jesse in Bethlehem and told him, "I will show you which of Jesse's sons you are to anoint for Me."

Samuel met with Jesse and subtly sized up his sons. The first one he met, Eliab, was impressive. He was the firstborn and had the look of a king. *This must be the one,* Samuel thought to himself, but God interrupted his train of thought.

> Do not look at his appearance or at his physical stature, because I have refused him. For the LORD does not see as man sees; for man looks at the outward appearance, but the LORD looks at the heart.
> —1 SAMUEL 16:7

Jesse introduced his next son, Abinadab, to Samuel, but God again told Samuel that he wasn't the future king either. One by one, Jesse's sons passed before Samuel—seven in all—but none of them were *the* one.

"Don't you have any more sons?" Samuel asked Jesse in desperation. Jesse thought for a moment, counted on his fingers, looked around the room at his sons, and then his eyes lit up. "Oh yes, I forgot about David, my youngest son. He's out in the fields watching the sheep."

"Well, send someone out to get him," Samuel replied. "We won't sit down to eat until he gets here." By this point, it was getting late in the day, and Samuel was getting hungry.

When David entered the room, he didn't look at all like what Samuel was expecting. He was a nice-looking boy—but still very much a boy. But what Samuel couldn't stop looking at was the boy's red hair! The person he was about to anoint as the next king of Israel was a red-haired, freckle-faced kid!

> *God has a way of taking people who have been rejected by society and raising them up into anointed, responsible men and women in positions of spiritual authority.*

Growing up as the last-born in the family, David knew what it meant to be the low man on the totem pole. He had to wear the hand-me-downs from seven brothers. He sat at the end of the table and was left to eat what his older brothers had passed over. He was the tagalong kid whom the brothers didn't always want to have around. And he was usually stuck doing the chores that none of his other brothers wanted to do—like watching sheep.

REJECTION PRODUCES COMPASSION

GOD HAS A way of taking people who have been rejected by society and raising them up into anointed, responsible men and women in positions of spiritual authority.

I tend to prefer those types of people because when they get into power, they're not nearly as arrogant as those who think they deserve to be there. They're usually not as self-righteous. They tend to be a little bit warmer and friendlier. They tend to reach out and embrace you because they understand that if it had not been for the Lord, they wouldn't be who they are and wouldn't have what they have.

When God raises you up, you have compassion for those around you. You look for those whom you can help because at one time, you were one of them.

David was probably the most down-to-earth king Israel ever had because he didn't grow up with a silver spoon in his mouth. He understood how it felt to work at one of the lowliest jobs a person could do at that time—he was a shepherd. David wasn't content walking around in purple robes, living in palaces and experiencing the finer things that go with being a king—especially when he knew someone was in trouble.

> *When God raises you up, you have compassion for the people around you, and you look for those whom you can help because at one time, you were one of them.*

AN UNEXPECTED WELCOME

DAVID WAS NOT only down-to-earth, but he also had a high regard for friendship. The covenant relationship David and Jonathan had was so strong that even after Jonathan was dead and David was ruling as king of Israel, David still honored his friend.

One day David said to himself, *I'm not happy to be blessed by myself. I want to find someone from Jonathan's family whom I can bless, too.*

After doing a little research, David learned there was

a man named Ziba—formerly a servant of Jonathan's father, King Saul—who was still around and might be of help. David called Ziba to the royal palace and asked him, "Is there anyone left from the house of Saul whom I can bless on behalf of Jonathan?"

"As a matter of fact there is," Ziba replied. "Jonathan's son Mephibosheth is living in Lo Debar."

"Well, go get him and bring him here," David said.

As Ziba walked out of the king's court, David called his servants together and gave them instructions to begin preparations for the man's arrival. "We're going to have a party for Mephibosheth!" David announced.

The day of Mephibosheth's arrival finally came. Everything in the palace was ready. The people were in their places. And when they heard the sound of footsteps coming up to the door, David stood up to greet his guest.

As the door opened, Ziba walked in carrying a young man who was obviously disabled. David looked at him. "Mephibosheth? Is that you?"

Ziba set the young man down, who then prostrated himself before the king. "Here is your servant," announced Ziba.

David picked him up, held him in his arms and said, "Don't be afraid of me. I loved your father, Jonathan, so much that I want to bring you into my palace and treat you like my own son."

Mephibosheth didn't look at all as David had expected. He didn't look like his father, Jonathan, and he certainly didn't look anything like his grandfather Saul. The look of aristocracy was gone. He was simply a trembling, frail, broken, bent-out-of-shape young man who had to be carried in by another person.

MORE THAN WHAT MEETS THE EYE

HOW DO *YOU* treat people who don't measure up to the yardstick of your expectations?

I'm not speaking in terms of appearance necessarily. I'm talking about character flaws. Perhaps they're the kind of people who are a little more dependent, or those who need a little more attention or affection. Maybe they just seem to be social misfits. You may wonder how they got to be that way.

But you don't know what they've been through. You can't judge a book by its cover, and you certainly can't evaluate a person only by what you can see.

Second Samuel 4 tells us how Mephibosheth inherited his physical condition. When Mephibosheth was five years old, his father and grandfather were killed in battle. Afraid that the death of the king might cause an insurrection, his nurse picked him up and fled the capital to prevent the boy—at that time a legal heir to the throne—from being assassinated.

While rushing out of the city, the nurse dropped Mephibosheth, and his feet were severely injured. Without the benefit of modern medicine, his feet didn't heal properly. As a result, Mephibosheth was crippled for the rest of his life.

WHAT TO DO
WHEN YOU'VE BEEN DROPPED

WHEN YOU ENCOUNTER people who don't act as you think they should—maybe they require a little more attention and time—there's a chance that someone dropped them.

> *When you encounter people who don't act as you think they should—maybe they require a little more attention and time—there's a chance that someone dropped them.*

On the surface they may seem to be a little different. They're deep thinkers, or they read their Bibles longer and fast more often. Perhaps they're always in need of prayer or they struggle with the same problems week after week. Don't judge them by their appearance or behavior. Samuel eventually didn't. David didn't. God doesn't.

Do you know what it is like to have people drop you at a time when you are vulnerable, at a time when you thought you could depend on them? Do you know what it is like to have something occur in your life that is so devastating, so overwhelming that it cripples you for the rest of your life?

You may even be one of those people.

Your spirit has been wounded. Something happened in your life that is so personal, so hurtful, that you can't even talk about it. You know you should be further along in your spiritual maturity or your emotional security, but someone dropped you. And inside you wonder, *Does anyone even care about me? Does anyone see how much I'm hurting?*

You've been dropped, and the devil has decided, "I'm going to use this situation to keep this man from fulfilling his destiny. I'm going to use this wound to keep this woman from being a woman of prayer. I'm going to use this painful memory to keep this person from putting me under his feet."

When you've been dropped, you need special care and special attention. When you've been dropped, you may *have* to pray a little longer; you may have to reach a little further.

There are pastors who have been dropped by people in their churches. There are people who have been dropped by their pastors. No one is exempt from experiencing the emotional pain of being dropped. Wounds touch every area of society: rich, poor, famous, unknown, man, woman, red, yellow, black and white. While we live in this world, we can experience pain that can deeply wound and scar us for life.

GETTING OUT OF LO DEBAR

IT WASN'T MEPHIBOSHETH'S fault that he had been dropped. But there he was sitting on the floor of the king's palace, unable to reach his personal potential because of past injuries.

Mephibosheth had spent the bulk of his life in the town of Lo Debar. Lo Debar means "pastureless," and it represents the place of desolation, loneliness and alienation.

The enemy wants people who have been wounded and rejected to live there. He wants them feeling desolate, lonely and alienated without any hope of being healed or freed from the pain of the past.

But I have good news for those who live in Lo Debar: There is a power that can get you out.

The Bible says that King David sent some men to bring Mephibosheth out of Lo Debar. If the responsibility were up to Mephibosheth, he would have never left because he was unable to walk out on his own.

When you've been crippled, you can't walk away from your past on your own. You need someone to pick you up and carry you out of your Lo Debar, your place of woundedness and alienation.

Thank God that the Holy Ghost makes house calls! The Holy Ghost will find you and pick you up when everybody else has forgotten about you or walked right past you because of your problem.

> *The Holy Ghost will find you and pick you up when everybody else has forgotten about you or walked right past you because of your problem.*

Jesus told His disciples, "It is to your advantage that I go away; for if I do not go away, the Helper will not come to you" (John 16:7). The Greek word for helper is *paraclete,* which means "to come to one's aid" or "to come alongside."

God gave you the Holy Ghost to pick you up when you fall down. He gave you the Holy Ghost to carry you out of Lo Debar when you can't walk out on your own. He gave you the Holy Ghost to come alongside and tell you, "Your past has no bearing on your future because in the name of Jesus your future is bright and bursting with hope! So don't give up. Don't isolate yourself. Stand tall." The Holy Spirit will pick you up and say, "When you get weary, you can lean on Me because that's why God sent me!"

Here's what God says about the ministry of the Holy Ghost:

The Spirit of the Lord GOD is upon Me,
Because the LORD has anointed Me
To preach good tidings to the poor;
He has sent Me to heal the brokenhearted,
To proclaim liberty to the captives,
And the opening of the prison to those who are
    bound;
To proclaim the acceptable year of the LORD,
And the day of vengeance of our God;
To comfort all who mourn,
To console those who mourn in Zion,
To give them beauty for ashes,
The oil of joy for mourning,
The garment of praise for the spirit of heaviness;
That they may be called trees of righteousness,
The planting of the LORD, that He may be glori-
    fied.

                            —ISAIAH 61:1–3

The Holy Spirit anoints us, heals our broken hearts, proclaims liberty to us when we are captive and opens the prison doors that lock us in. When you're held hostage by the hurts and rejection of the past, the Holy Ghost can storm the gates that the devil locked shut and rescue you.

The Spirit also comforts us, consoles us and clothes us with the garment of praise in exchange for the heaviness that surrounded us for so long. And when the Holy Spirit is finished with us, people will call us "trees of righteousness, the planting of the Lord, that He may be glorified."

But God isn't content simply healing us. He also

wants to return to us what was stolen. Let's look at the very next verse:

> And they shall rebuild the old ruins,
> They shall raise up the former desolations,
> And they shall repair the ruined cities,
> The desolations of many generations.
> —ISAIAH 61:4

God not only delivers you from the Lo Debars in your life, but He also goes back to them and rebuilds them. God doesn't release you from your past so you can walk forward and never look back again. God wants you to look back and see your past through the healing power of Jesus Christ. He wants you to remember how far you've come.

> *God not only delivers you from the Lo Debars in your life, but He also goes to go back to them and rebuilds them.*

Can you imagine moving back to Lo Debar after it's been rebuilt? What used to be a dry, desolate ghost town is now a thriving, prosperous city. The dirt roads have been paved. The grass has been watered and mowed. So you decide to walk down the street to the corner drugstore where you used to sit alone drinking a Coke, feeling sorry for yourself. The building is still there, but it's been remodeled into a youth center where teenagers can go after school. You can walk back through the old building, but it's just not the same.

God wants us to remember the past, but He wants to

heal us so completely that we no longer have a past to return *to*. And we wouldn't want to go back anyway. But He wants us to always remember how far we've come.

> *God wants us to remember the past, but He wants to heal us in such a way that we no longer have a past to return to.*

GOD'S SPECIAL BLESSINGS

THERE IS ONE part of the story about Mephibosheth that used to bother me. Nowhere do you read that Mephibosheth got healed. I wondered what joy could there be for a crippled boy to limp in pain all his life?

But as I prayed about it, God impressed me with this: People who aren't sick don't need a physician. Mephibosheth's injury caused him to need God, and it was his need of God that caused God to bless him.

God has a special blessing for the crippled child because when he's weak, then God is strong. The more he needs God, the more God strengthens him. The more he leans on God, the more God holds him up.

But most importantly, David adopted Mephibosheth. David took a poor, crippled boy who was an outcast living in a desolate cow town and gave him a seat at the king's table with the rest of David's family.

Best of all, Mephibosheth didn't even have to go outside and work in the fields. All his needs were supplied by the king. When other folks were trying to work up a blessing, Mephibosheth just sat back and enjoyed feasting at the king's table.

When God raises you up, it doesn't matter who looks at you funny or who thinks you should be sitting at the king's table. When God brings you there, you have just as much a right to be there as anyone else.

GOD SEES THROUGH OUR REJECTION AND HURT

AFTER DAVID WELCOMED him into his family, Mephibosheth responded by saying, "What is your servant, that you should look upon such a dead dog as I?" (2 Sam. 9:8). In other words, "Why would you take an interest in someone who can't even support himself? I've been hurt. Can't you see my scars? I'm damaged merchandise, a reject of society who can't do anything for himself."

How many of us respond in the same way when we've been rejected and hurt? "God, I'm nothing but a dead dog. I've messed up. Other people have messed me up, and now I'm damaged merchandise. Why would You ever want to use me?"

But God says, "You're not who you think you are. You're the righteousness of God in Christ. My Son Jesus died on the cross to free you from your bondage to rejection and low self-esteem. And because you belong to Me, you're more than what the devil says about you. You can go farther and do more than what the devil says you can do. My divine power has given to you *all* things that pertain to life and godliness. I'm the God of new beginnings and second chances."

The devil is a liar. His decision for your life is to fool you into thinking you aren't anything. He wants you walking around in pain. He wants you living in Lo Debar, dwelling on the hurts of the past. But God has a different plan for your life.

Chapter 15

You Were Created for a Purpose

VAGABONDS ARE VAGUE people who wander through life without accomplishing anything. They are always moving around—no roots, no commitment. If you ask them about their purpose in life, their faces look deader than four o'clock. When you live without purpose, the devil can throw anything in front of you to dominate your thoughts and distract you from knowing Christ.

Recently I noticed that Satan attacks some people in a very subtle way by getting them to be vague about their lives. He wants them to live without any definite thoughts or ideas or plans for the future. It is dangerous because if you have no purpose, Satan will give you one.

Some of Satan's decisions for our lives are pretty obvious: poverty, sickness, strife, rebellion. But purpose-lessness is one of the devil's decisions that is overlooked by many Christians, one I am going to explain in this chapter.

> *If you have no purpose, Satan will give you one.*

In the Christian life, we're either moving forward in faith against the devil, or he's chasing us and we're on the run. We need to get over the mind-set that says we can live in the gray areas of life and do neither. If we neglect to live purposeful lives, we will surely find ourselves on the run.

PEOPLE WITH PURPOSE

WE NEED TO be a people who do what we do with purpose. Rather than waiting for the will of God to fall on us, we need to find it on purpose.

You may be a man or woman of strong purpose, but it may be the wrong purpose.

Some people spend their whole lives climbing the ladder of success, only to discover when they get to the top that their ladder is leaning against the wrong building. They might have had a strong sense of purpose, but in the end it profited them nothing.

The number one purpose for every born-again believer ought to be Philippians 3:10, "That I may know Him and the power of His resurrection, and the fellowship of His sufferings, being conformed to His death."

It's not enough to go to church every week. You have to *know* Jesus, not merely know *about* Jesus, but truly know Him. We know Him in the joy of His resurrection—we experience His healing and His saving and delivering power in our lives every day. We also know Him through His sufferings. When we die to our fleshly desires and habits, we can come to know Him.

If you're going to know Him in His death and resurrection, it means you're going to have to direct a good portion of your time toward Him. Knowing Jesus doesn't just happen. We don't naturally grow deeper in our walk with God. Knowing Jesus happens on purpose.

WHAT PURPOSE IS

THE DICTIONARY DEFINES *purpose* as "the object toward which one strives or for which something exists."[1]

Jesus understood His purpose, and He existed to fulfill it. The Bible tells us, "For this purpose the Son of God was manifested, that He might destroy the works of the devil" (1 John 3:8). Jesus' sole purpose for coming to earth was to destroy the stranglehold of sin and death in which the devil held us.

> *Jesus' sole purpose for coming to earth was to destroy the stranglehold of sin and death in which the devil held us.*

So what are you striving for? Why do you exist?

Sometimes we strive to do what everybody else is doing so we can be a part of the right group and not be rejected. But that only brings frustration, and in the process, we miss the purpose God has for us.

GOD'S CALL ON YOUR LIFE

DO YOU KNOW why I'm happy even though I work very hard? It's because I'm doing what God has called me to do. The only way that you're going to be happy and fulfilled is if you find what God wants for you and pour yourself into it 100 percent.

> *The only way that you're going to be happy and fulfilled is if you find what God wants for you and pour yourself into it 100 percent.*

Now you might think, "Well, I'm not called to full-time ministry."

But you're called to something. God has a call on every person's life. It may be full-time ministry, but then again it may be digging ditches. All jobs are equally valid in God's eyes, and each one of us should find some sense of satisfaction and purpose in accomplishing our work.

Some people, however, are vague. They don't know what they're doing. They're not going anywhere and they don't even have a plan.

There's one more definition of *purpose* I'd like to look at: "To intend or resolve to perform or accomplish."

That means, if you're going to have a purpose, you're going to have to go out and do it on purpose. It's not going to just happen.

Now let's look at the definition of the word *vague:* "Not clearly expressed. Not thinking or expressing oneself clearly. Lacking definite shape, form or character."[2]

Take a moment and ask yourself which word—*purposeful* or *vague*—best describes you. Does your life seem foggy, fuzzy, hazy, indefinite, indistinct, misty or unclear? Or do you know who you are, where you're headed and what your purpose is?

BEING A CHRISTIAN ON PURPOSE

ANYBODY CAN BE a Christian, but you have to make your mind up to be a good one. The church doesn't need any more part-time believers.

> *Anybody can be a Christian, but you have to make your mind up to be a good one.*

If you're going to serve God, serve Him with your whole heart. Don't just serve Him when you're desperate or in trouble and then ignore Him the rest of the time.

God says in Jeremiah 29:13, "You will seek me and find me when you seek me with all your heart" (NIV). Until we say, "God, I want You so badly that I'm willing to do anything to have You," we won't see God. He has to be our all-consuming passion.

Being a Christian on purpose requires the dedication and determination to cut off some of the other things in your life that are either not bearing good fruit or just wasting your time.

IF WE DO OUR PART, GOD WILL DO HIS

FINDING GOD'S WILL doesn't just happen. If you want to

stay in the will of God you have to be determined. Determined means to dig in both heels and say to yourself, "It doesn't matter what I feel or see; I'm getting in the will of God."

Vague people, on the other hand, say to themselves, "I sure wish I knew God's will for my life."

The good news is, we can know God's will, but it might require a little work. Ephesians 5:14 says:

> Therefore He says, Awake, O sleeper, and arise from the dead, and Christ shall shine (make day dawn) upon you and give you light.
>
> —AMP

This passage of Scripture instructs the believer that if you do this, then God will do that. If you awake, Christ will make your day dawn and give you light. In other words, once you get up from doing nothing, God will begin giving you direction to move ahead.

So here's a little insight into how God works: If you do your part, God will surely do His.

If you do your part, God will surely do His.

TAKE INVENTORY

Look carefully then how you walk!

—EPHESIANS 5:15, AMP

Spend thirty minutes sometime, taking an inventory of your life. Ask yourself, *Where am I going, and what am I doing?*

You may come out saying, *This is what I am doing: I am in the center of God's will for me right now, and I am pressing forward the best I know how.* If that is true for your life, then keep up the good work!

You also may come out saying, *Have I got a mess on my hands!* With a clearer picture of what you are dealing with, you can then begin making changes.

But last of all, you may also come up with a vague answer like, *I'm not sure what I'm doing!* You do one thing this one week, something else another week, this today, that tomorrow, flopping back and forth, never having any real direction.

But we are exhorted, "Look carefully how you walk!" That means, pay attention to what you're doing and how you're spending your time because you don't have any time to waste. God has a plan for your life. He wants to use you. You're important—in your neighborhood, in the church, in the marketplace.

If you don't do any thing but get into the marketplace and live your Christian testimony before every person you come into contact with, then you are doing your job quite well. But to do that, you have to get serious about developing the character of Jesus Christ so you don't act like the rest of the world and hurt the cause of Christ.

If God didn't need us after we were born again, He'd just beam us up and our lives would be over with. He doesn't leave us here to see how miserable we can be. He leaves us here so we can do what Jesus did, so we can develop and become mature. When we do that, we show forth the glory of God.

> *If God didn't need us after we were born again, He'd just beam us up and our lives would be over with.*

Unbelievers aren't reading Bibles to find out about Jesus; they are reading you and me. Your life is telling a story, so be careful how you walk. Pay attention to how you act in public.

LIVE PURPOSEFULLY

> Live purposefully and worthily and accurately, not as the unwise and witless, but as wise (sensible, intelligent people).
>
> —EPHESIANS 5:15, AMP

Live purposefully. That means to do what you know you ought to do on purpose, not just because it is convenient or you fall into it. This is where many people get vague.

Sometimes Satan seems to throw a spirit of vagueness over people so they are indecisive and lack any direction or purpose. They just sit around wishing something good would happen. "I sure wish I knew what God wanted me to do."

Paul, on the other hand, wrote, "I do not run like a man running aimlessly; I do not fight like a man beating the air" (1 Cor. 9:26, NIV). Paul didn't wait for life to happen because he knew if he did, it would pass him by.

Make the Most of Your Time

Making the very most of the time [buying up each opportunity], because the days are evil.
—Ephesians 5:16, AMP

We need to be careful how we spend every minute. I'm not saying we have to be doing something every second of every day. We all need time for rest and play. But the breaks in our work should come because we planned them. Wasting time, however, takes no planning whatsoever. If I'm not careful, it just happens. Nothing aggravates me more than to come to the end of a day and realize that I have accomplished absolutely nothing.

The biggest and most avoidable time wasters are those segments of time—fifteen, twenty or thirty minutes—in between meetings or activities. By the end of the day we lose hours of precious time just waiting. But if we live purposefully, making the very most of every minute, we'll be able to identify those drains of time and learn to make them productive, too.

Purpose Includes Commitment

Therefore do not be vague and thoughtless and foolish, but understanding and firmly grasping what the will of the Lord is.
—Ephesians 5:17, AMP

Paul is saying in this verse, "You need to know what the will of the Lord is, not just a general idea of God's will, but the kind of understanding you can hold onto with both hands. You need to know it and understand it and feel it." So how can you know what the will of the Lord is?

He's obviously saying here that if you're vague, you're never going to find out the will of God for your life. First, you must stop being vague.

Next, begin to step out. So many people want God to open the door for them before they take any steps. But you'll never know if it really *is* God until you step out and start doing what He tells you to do. Stepping out means more than just sticking your toe in the water. You need commitment. If you aren't committed, then the first time you encounter a wave, you'll jump back onto the shore.

I can warn you from experience that not everything God tells you to do is going to be easy. As a matter of fact, He'll throw something in the water every once in a while just to see if you'll stay in there. But in the process you'll stretch and grow. So don't be afraid of commitment.

You'll never find purpose in something you aren't committed to. As believers, we need to be people who say what we are going to do and then do what we say.

We also can't be people who shy away from a job because it's difficult. Where would we be if Jesus started carrying that cross up the hill and said, "Oh, forget it Father, this is too hard." Isn't He our example?

Too many people wade around in the shallow water all their life, always choosing to play it safe. Peter was the only one who walked on the water, but he was also the only one that took a chance on drowning. People who always play it safe seldom end up in the perfect will of God.

FINDING GOD'S WILL

IF PURPOSE COMES from finding God's will, then how do we find God's will for our lives? There are two concerns I would caution you about:

First, don't just jump onto every hair-brained idea that comes along. As we've already discussed in a previous chapter, wait on God, but don't make a ministry out of waiting.

> **Wait on God, but don't make a ministry out of waiting.**

Can you ever know for certain that an idea is from God? I don't think so. If the idea were 100 percent certain, then it wouldn't require any faith.

And what happens if you're wrong? You'll survive it.

Second, if you step out into something and you know right away that it's wrong, be quick to admit it. Don't let your pride get in the way to where you end up trying to make it look like God when it's not.

Here are some additional keys to help you be certain you're in God's perfect will:

- *You know the idea is not of God if the door doesn't open.* If the doors keep closing, don't try to kick them open. When God is in it, there's going to be grace on it. Grace is the ability the Holy Spirit gives you to do what you could not do for yourself.

- *You know the idea is not of God if you don't sense any peace.* That doesn't mean you won't have any opposition. But you must have that sense of peace in your inner man so you will have the courage to continue when opposition does come.

- *You know the idea is not of God if the provision isn't there.* If God is calling you to do something and it requires money, then God is going to provide the resources in order to accomplish it.

- *Does your idea make good use of your spiritual gifts?*

One of first places to start in seeking God's will for your life is to evaluate the spiritual gifts that He has already given to you. He won't give you any gift that He doesn't want you to use.

We need to give ourselves to our spiritual gifts. If your gift is teaching, give yourself to teaching. If your gift is exhorting, give yourself to exhorting. If your gift is helping, then you ought to find whomever it is that God wants you to help so you can help them.

GIVING YOURSELF TO GOD'S PURPOSES

BEFORE I BRING this chapter to a close, I want to look at one more passage of Scripture.

> I appeal to you therefore, brethren, and beg of you in view of [all] the mercies of God, to make a decisive dedication of your bodies [presenting all your members and faculties] as a living sacrifice.
> —ROMANS 12:1, AMP

God wants us to make a decisive dedication of our bodies. We need to choose willingly to go anywhere and do anything when God calls us. There are people struggling with purposelessness in their lives who aren't willing to do anything about it. And they don't even realize that the purpose they are looking for lies in the very things they are avoiding.

Decisively dedicating our bodies also includes our mouths. We have to be selective in what we say. Often, we can talk ourselves right out of God's blessing and direction.

> Do not be conformed to this world (this age), [fashioned after and adapted to its external, superficial customs], but be transformed (changed) by the [entire] renewal of your mind [by its new ideals and it's new attitude].
>
> —ROMANS 12:2, AMP

God doesn't want just our bodies; He wants our minds as well. We need to decide what we're going to think about and what we're not going to think about. If we want God's direction for our lives, then we have to be willing to program our minds with the renewing, transforming Word of God.

> So that you may prove [for yourselves] what is the good and acceptable and perfect will of God.
>
> —ROMANS 12:2, AMP

We prove for ourselves what is the good and acceptable and perfect will of God. God doesn't prove it for us. You have to be willing to try Him. Take some risks. Be willing to make some mistakes. To prove God's will you may even have to go through some experiences that you would prefer not to go through.

The devil wants us lacking in purpose. He wants us facing our lives without any idea where we are going so that He can lead us away from the blessings of God. The devil will do whatever he can to keep us from stepping out and finding the purpose that comes from fulfilling God's will for our lives.

God wants to deliver His people from vagueness. But God won't *make* you do anything. He'll show you what He'd like you to do, but you will still have to do the "doing." He'll give you the strength, but you'll still have to do the doing. You've got a part, and God's got a part. You do your part, and He'll do His!

Chapter 16

Breaking Through, Not Breaking Down

THERE WILL COME times when your own shield of faith has so many darts in it that you feel you can't hold it up any more. You look your shield over, and there isn't room for another dart. Sometimes you'll be so tired and battle-worn you feel that you can't stand anymore. When the enemy has surrounded you for months or even years, and your shield of faith is full of darts and you feel you can't carry it much further, then you get hit by one final blow—the grand finale of them all. But don't you dare give up! You're at the point of your breakthrough. Let me explain.

After King Saul had been killed in battle, the people of Israel approached David and asked him to be their king. David and the elders made a covenant before God, and he was then anointed king of Israel just as God had promised through Samuel.

Israel's favorite son was finally fulfilling his life's purpose!

THE ANOINTING ATTRACTS ATTACK

And when the Philistines heard that David was anointed king...

—1 CHRONICLES 14:8, AMP

When we commit our lives to Christ, the Bible tells us that God anoints us. John wrote, "But you have an anointing from the Holy One, and you know all things" (1 John 2:20). The anointing *sets apart* and *imparts*. It *sets apart* a person for a particular work or service, and it *imparts* into that person a supernatural strength and authority that he or she didn't have previously. As Christians, we have a measure of authority in the spiritual realm that makes angels stand at attention, demons tremble and most of all, Satan takes notice.

> *The anointing... sets apart a person for a particular work or service, and it imparts into that person a supernatural strength and authority that he or she didn't have previously.*

The moment God makes real in your spirit the power of the anointing in your life, it changes the way you live. You get bold and aggressive. You do things that you would never have done before. You talk as you have never talked before. You really believe that Satan cannot defeat you anymore. And the stronger the anointing gets, the bolder you become.

The devil knows what kind of trouble is ahead of him

when he comes against a believer who walks in the anointing. Knowing that the best defense is a good offense, he makes you a target.

Just because the anointing is in you and on you doesn't mean that you're just going to coast through life without any challenges. The anointing makes you dangerous.

The Philistines have always served as a symbol or type of the enemies of God and His people. Today our enemy is not flesh and blood, but rather principalities, powers, rulers of darkness and wicked spirits in high places—all of Satan's powerful instruments. These forces of evil hate you, and they hate what you stand for.

When you begin to recognize that the anointing of God is in you and that you have access to the same anointing and power that Jesus operated in, you can bet that the Philistines are going to hear about it and challenge you.

It happened to David. Everything was going well for the young ruler. Israel had affirmed his leadership. He had just been anointed king. This was a great time in his life that he, like any person in his position, would want to enjoy. After just getting started, however, the Philistines mobilized an attack. Satan loves to launch his severest attacks right after you have experienced a major victory in your life. You can never drop your guard. You can never go on a spiritual vacation, take off your armor, pile it over in a corner somewhere and say, "I don't want to play this faith stuff anymore; the last faith project almost killed me. I need a break." You can't take a vacation or a holiday from your faith life.

> *Satan loves to launch his severest attacks right after you have experienced a major victory in your life.*

The Bible says the just shall live by faith. (See Hebrews 10:38.) You don't get up in the morning wondering if you're going to live by faith or not. It's your lifestyle.

So, it was a wonderful time of victory in David's life, and right in the middle of it the Philistines launched an attack—a major challenge. Satan, the thief, came immediately to steal. Don't think for one moment that Satan is going to roll over and play dead and allow you to receive all the revelation you need and not confront you. He might challenge you immediately, he might wait awhile, but he *will* challenge you regarding the Word you have received. I promise you, the Philistines will hear about the anointing on your life, and they *will* launch an attack.

THE LORD OF BREAKING THROUGH

NOW NOTICE WHAT David did.

> And when the Philistines heard that David was anointed king over all Israel, [they] all went up to seek David. And [he] heard of it and went out before them.... David asked God, Shall I go up against the Philistines? And will you deliver them into my hand? And the Lord said, Go up, and I will deliver them into your hand.
>
> —1 CHRONICLES 14:8, 10, AMP

219

David didn't run from his enemies. The anointing on your life does not cause you to retreat; it gives you the confidence to attack. No longer are you satisfied living on the defensive; instead you go on the offensive. You become militant and unwilling to take anything from the devil anymore. You stand in his face, toe to toe, and tell him, "If it's a fight you want, it's a fight you're going to get. But when the dust settles, God and I will be the last ones standing!"

> So [Israel] came up to Baal-perazim, and David smote [the Philistines] there. Then David said, God has broken my enemies by my hand, like the bursting forth of waters. Therefore they called the name of that place Baal-perazim [Lord of breaking through].
>
> —1 CHRONICLES 14:11, AMP

After David and the armies of Israel successfully defeated the Philistines, the people named the place Baal-perazim, which means in Hebrew, "Lord of breaking through." David walked in the anointing that God placed upon his life and found that he could depend upon God when he needed a breakthrough.

God is the *Lord of the breakthrough*. That's one of His names.

When the devil has decided that you should live in sickness, God has a *healing* name. When the devil has decided that you should live in turmoil and anxiety, God has a *peace* name. When the devil has decided that you should live in a spiritual or physical blockage or impasse, God has a *breakthrough* name. The Lord of the breakthrough always comes through for one of His own!

> *The Lord of the breakthrough always comes through for one of His own!*

ONE WORD IS ALL YOU NEED

THE APOSTLE PAUL also discovered the Lord of the breakthrough. Paul was facing a potential catastrophe. The ship on which he was to travel was scheduled to leave from the port of Fair Havens bound for Phoenix on the island of Crete. But God had impressed upon him that the devil had other plans. If they set sail, their voyage would end in disaster and a potential loss of life. Paul had no choice in deciding whether or not to go because he also happened to be a prisoner bound for Rome.

Despite Paul's warnings to the people on board, the majority decided that the ship should sail ahead. And sure enough, a storm hit just as Paul had said. After days at sea without a break in the storm, Acts 27 tells us that all hope of being saved was lost. They needed a major miracle. They needed a major breakthrough.

We know that Paul was a praying man. We also know that he prayed in the Holy Ghost. He wrote in his letter to the Corinthian church, "I thank my God I speak with tongues more than you all" (1 Cor. 14:18). I'm confident that Paul was praying in the Holy Ghost out there on that ship.

At some point in the midst of the storm, God gave Paul a word. One word from God is all you need to change your circumstances. One word from God can bring a breakthrough!

221

One word from God can bring a breakthrough!

Paul prayed in the Holy Spirit, and God sent an angel who told him, "Don't be afraid. You're going to lose your ship and your supplies, but not a single life will be lost." Encouraged by the word God gave him, Paul shared it with the others on the boat, and just as he said, not one life was lost. A breakthrough.

Paul prayed in the Holy Ghost, and God gave him a word. God said, "No one on the boat is going to die." And that's all Paul needed to know. The Lord of the breakthrough came through, and He'll come through for you every time you need a breakthrough, too!

The Lord of the breakthrough came through, and He'll come through for you every time you need a breakthrough, too!

Praying in the Holy Ghost is one of the greatest keys to getting a breakthrough because praying in the Holy Ghost can cause a "God idea" to rise up within you. A God idea is more than a good idea. It is an anointed, God-breathed, God-inspired word of deliverance. My spirit attracts God ideas, and yours does, too. If you need a breakthrough, all you need is a God idea.

You're a Target

PAUL WAS ON his way to see the emperor of the Roman Empire where he was hoping to share the gospel. Satan knew what could happen if Paul actually had an opportunity to share with the emperor, so he did whatever he could to stop him. King David was a target, Paul was a target and Job was a target, too.

The Bible tells us Job was "blameless and upright, and one who feared God and shunned evil" (Job 1:1). He was a righteous man whom God blessed greatly. Obviously he had an anointing on his life. Then a catastrophe struck. Job described what happened:

> I was living at ease, but [Satan] crushed me and broke me apart; yes, he seized me by the neck and dashed me in pieces; *then he set me up for his target.*
> —JOB 16:12, AMP, EMPHASIS ADDED

Job was living in ease, he had money in the bank, he was enjoying good health, his marriage was strong, his kids were all serving the Lord, the refrigerator worked, nothing needed to be repaired, everything was going well—and then all hell broke loose.

> *If you're anointed, you're a target. The fact that Satan attacks you out of the blue is evidence that you are dangerous to him.*

If you're anointed, you're a target. The fact that Satan attacks you out of the blue is evidence that you are dangerous to him. You are a threat to his operation. So you are a target also. And if the devil never bothers you, then you aren't a threat.

Just because you are a target doesn't mean that you have to sit there and receive every fiery dart the devil throws your way. That's the reason you have been given the shield of faith. But there will come times when your own shield of faith has so many darts in it that you feel as if you can't hold it up any more. You look your shield over and see that there isn't room for one more dart.

Sometimes you're so tired and battle-worn you feel as if you can't stand anymore. When your shield of faith is full of darts, and you feel you can't carry it much further, don't you dare give up. There is a missile coming. And when that missile hits your shield, it may rock you; you don't know if you can stand anymore. But if you don't fall with this one... then it's all over. He's just fired his best shot, and you've won!

Job said, "I was living at ease, and suddenly I became a target of the devil." Let's look at how he responded.

WHERE TO GO TO GET THE WORD

My days are past, my purposes and plans are frustrated; even the thoughts (desires and possessions) of my heart are broken off.... Where then is my hope? And, if I have hope, who will see [its fulfillment]?

—JOB 17:11,15, AMP

Job was saying, "My life was going fine when suddenly I became a target for the devil. Everything I've tried in my own strength to overcome this attack hasn't worked. Now I'm frustrated. I feel my world is caving in around me. My back is against the wall. I've almost lost hope of ever coming out of this. I need a breakthrough."

Job wasn't even sure he was going to live through the attack to see his hope fulfilled.

What did David do when he needed a breakthrough? He inquired of the Lord. He asked God, "Shall I pursue this Philistine?" He sought the mind of God, and God gave him a God idea.

What did Job do?

> Then Job said to the Lord, I know that You can do all things, and that no thought or purpose of Yours can be restrained or thwarted.
>
> —JOB 42:1–2, AMP

He inquired of God. "You can do all things," Job said. He knew he needed the Lord of the breakthrough. Job sought the mind of God, and God told him to pray for his friends. He received a God idea. God spoke to Job's judgmental friends and told them:

> My servant Job shall pray for you, for I will accept [his prayer].
>
> —JOB 42:8, AMP

When David needed a breakthrough, God said, "Pursue." When Job needed a breakthrough, He said, "Pray for your friends." Two different words that produced two different breakthroughs for different attacks.

AN EVER-CHANGING WORD

AFTER DAVID AND the armies of Israel won that particular battle against the Philistines, the enemies came against him again. David inquired of God once more and asked, "Shall I pursue?" This time God answered, "No," and gave him an altogether different strategy that was just as successful. Two similar situations but two entirely different words. God may not tell you to do it the same way every time, but there is a God idea for every breakthrough.

> *God may not tell you to do it the same way every time, but there is a God idea for every breakthrough.*

If you pay close attention to Jesus' healing ministry, you notice that He dealt differently with every situation. Sometimes He spoke a word. Sometimes He laid His hands on people. On one occasion He spit on the ground, mixed the spittle and dirt into clay and put it on the man's eyes. Jesus varied His methods according to the direction of the Holy Ghost. I don't know why God chooses to do it this way. All I know is obedience is the key to the miraculous.

Once in the middle of a meeting, a great man of God invited a precious elderly man who had stomach ulcers to come up to the platform. Then, in front of the audience, he slugged the man in the stomach, knocking him to the floor. The audience was shocked, but the man stood up healed.

Now let me strongly suggest that you not go around hitting people and believing it is the anointing. You might get hit back. I also strongly suggest that you not spit on anybody. As a matter of fact, you better not do anything because you heard somebody else did it and got results. Do what God tells you to do, and you'll find your breakthrough.

There is a God idea for every breakthrough. And your spirit attracts God ideas. While you are driving down the highway, a God idea will drop into your spirit. While you are asleep at night, a God idea will drop into your spirit.

After Job prayed for his friends, God gave him a breakthrough and turned his captivity around.

> And the Lord turned the captivity of Job and restored his fortunes, when he prayed for his friends; also the Lord gave Job twice as much as he had before.... And the Lord blessed the latter days of Job more than his beginning.
>
> —JOB 42:10,12, AMP

Job's breakthrough came as a result of a God idea. Once God gives you a God idea and you act on it, the breakthrough comes.

Once God gives you a God idea and you act on it, the breakthrough comes.

GETTING THE GOD IDEA

FOR JOB AND David, the God idea came as a result of spending time in the presence of God. Breakthroughs come when you receive a word from God, and a word from God only comes when you spend time with Him. You can't watch television all day and expect to get a breakthrough.

> *Breakthroughs come when you receive a word from God, and a word from God only comes when you spend time with Him.*

God has an idea that will turn your business, or your ministry around. He has an idea that will cause your house that's been on the market for years to sell, or that will cause your child to come home.

When Satan sends a missile against you, it will take a God idea to turn the situation around. But you are not going to get it playing church and religious games. You're going to get it spending time with God.

WHERE TO FIND THE GOD IDEA

SPENDING TIME IN God's presence and praying in the Spirit is the way godly and skillful wisdom comes to you. Proverbs 2:6 says, "For the LORD gives wisdom; from His mouth come knowledge and understanding."

All the God ideas you will need from here until Jesus appears has been stored up for you. And they are as close to you as your next breath. Proverbs 2:7 tells us, "He stores up sound wisdom for the upright; he is a shield to those who walk uprightly."

If all the treasures of knowledge and wisdom are hidden in God, and Christ is in you, then all of the wisdom and God ideas you'll ever need are in your spirit man, where Christ is enthroned.

You don't have to depend on other people to hear from God. You don't have to attend a conference and listen to an anointed speaker so you can grab him or her after the service and ask, "What do you think I ought to do?" You're anointed. First John 2:27 says, "But the anointing which you have received from Him abides in you, and you do not need that anyone teach you." All the God ideas you need are already inside you.

> *All the God ideas you need are already inside you.*

Where are they? In your spirit. If you're desperate for a breakthrough, then spend time with God and draw them out.

Here is an important way to draw that God idea out of your spirit:

> For one who speaks in an [unknown] tongue speaks not to men but to God, for no one understands or catches his meaning, because in the [Holy] Spirit he utters secret truths and hidden things [not obvious to the understanding].
> —1 CORINTHIANS 14:2, AMP

When you are praying in the Holy Spirit, you are uttering secret truths and hidden things in another language out of your spirit. Your mind doesn't catch it, but your spirit draws it out and speaks it.

Therefore, the person who speaks in an [unknown] tongue should pray [for the power] to interpret and explain what it says.

—1 CORINTHIANS 14:13, AMP

Now I realize that the application of this verse is in a church setting, but that doesn't necessarily limit it to the church. Paul is saying that when you are praying in church and people are speaking in tongues, pray that you may interpret so everyone can understand.

But you can't limit this verse to a church setting because people pray in tongues outside of church. I pray in the Spirit in my car, in my house and everywhere I go. I pray in the Spirit throughout the day. And if I can interpret what I have said in the Spirit in church, why can't I interpret what I have said in the Spirit in my car and my house?

If someone gives an utterance in tongues and someone else interprets it, what did we get? The meaning of the hidden thing was revealed so our minds could understand it.

That's why Paul encourages us to seek to interpret what we are praying in the Spirit. Here's what I do. I pray in the Spirit long enough to quiet my thoughts—so I don't hear what my mind says—and then I pray that I might interpret.

All it takes is one idea from God to change every negative situation in your life.

What's happening? I'm quieting my mind down so the Holy Ghost can have an opportunity to speak.

There are many other ways to receive that powerful word from God. Some pray in tongues and receive an interpretation; some read along in the Bible, and certain words seem to jump off the page at them. These words always are accompanied by the assurance that God has spoken something very direct and personal to their situation. Some kneel quietly in prayer, and in the peace of God's presence, they get an inner witness of what they should do. Some even receive a powerful prophetic word to accompany what God has spoken into their spirit. Regardless of how you receive it, you will have a blessed assurance that it is the hidden wisdom of God revealed to your understanding. You have prayed out a God idea that will produce your breakthrough.

Jesus said in John 7:38, "He who believes in Me, as the Scripture has said, out of his heart will flow rivers of living water." The Message translation puts it this way, "Rivers of living water will brim and spill out of the depths…"

Deep calls unto deep. This living water that comes out of your spirit is the wisdom of God. It's the God idea.

How desperate are you for a breakthrough? How badly do you want to reverse the devil's decision for your life? It's as close as the words of your mouth.

Pray in the Spirit and read the Word of God every day. Once you hear your God idea, then things will start changing. All it takes is one idea from God to change every negative situation in your life.

Now thank God, because it's breakthrough time!

Chapter 17

Reverse the Devil's Decision in Your Life

J ESUS ONCE TOLD the story about a farmer who went out to the field to plant seeds for the next year's crop. Back and forth he walked across the field, scattering seeds as he went. Some of the seeds fell along the path and were quickly eaten up by the birds. Other seeds were scattered onto the rocky areas. Those seeds sprang up quickly, but because the soil was shallow, the hot sun dried them up. Still other seeds were planted among the thorns. Again, the seeds grew, but the thorns choked off the plants. Finally, seeds were planted in fertile soil and then produced a crop yielding a return of up to one hundred times what was planted. (See Matthew 13:2–23.)

Jesus later explained to His disciples the meaning of His parable:

- The seed sown on the path represents people who hear the Word, but the devil snatches the seeds away.

- The seed on the rocky path represents the person who hears the Word and initially responds, but when trouble arises, he or she quickly falls away.

- The seed sown among the thorns represents people who hear the Word, but the lure of the things of this world choke off the Word.

- Finally, the seed sown on fertile soil represents the person who hears the Word, understands it and puts it to work in his life.

This parable of Jesus gives a good way of explaining how you can respond to the biblical principles you have read in this book.

You can be like the seed sown on the path. You may set this book down and never think about it again. There may be, however, some decisions the devil has made for your life that you will continue to struggle with again and again and wonder why.

You can be like the seed sown on the rocky places. You may finish the book and say, "Wow! God really spoke to me in that book. I can see some decisions the devil has made in my life that need to be reversed." But as you work to reverse the devil's decision, the attack it generates or the long wait it requires finally wears you down and you give up.

You can be like the seed sown among the thorns. The principles in this book challenge and inspire you to reverse the various decisions the devil has made for your life. But as you realize the sinful habits and wrong attitudes you may have to give up along the way, you decide it isn't worth it.

Or you can be like the seed sown on the fertile soil. As the Holy Spirit speaks to you through this book and empowers you to reverse the devil's decision for your life, the fruit of your efforts yield victory, healing and an ever-increasing anointing of the Holy Ghost in your life. Even if it takes longer than you thought or is more difficult than you planned, you're still in there fighting to reverse Satan's decision. You're not quitting, and you're not giving up.

Which one of the four are you? My hope is that you'll pick the last one.

God has chosen you for victory and blessing, but the decisions the devil has made for your life may be standing in the way. Your choice in accepting or reversing the devil's decision will determine whether or not you will experience the abundant life that God promises every Christian.

Take a look at the list below and ask yourself, *Do any of these areas represent decisions the devil has made in my life?*

- Anger
- Disease
- Envy
- Fear
- Hatred
- Low self-image
- Pride
- Purposelessness

- Discouragement
- Drug or alcohol addiction
- Failure
- Greed
- Laziness
- Poverty
- Profanity
- Rejection

- Sexual perversion
- Sorcery
- Unforgiveness
- Sickness
- Unemployment
- Unsaved loved ones

Of course, this is just a partial list.

If you can identify any of the items above as decisions you need to reverse, what steps are you going to take to reverse them? If you're unsure what to do next, you might want to review sections two and three again.

Because God is able to empower you to reverse every decision the devil has made for your life, I leave with you a word of encouragement from God's Word.

> Now to Him who is able to do exceedingly abundantly above all that we ask or think, according to the power that works in us, to Him be glory in the church by Christ Jesus to all generations, forever and ever. Amen.
>
> —EPHESIANS 3:20–21

The power of God is mightier than all the forces of the devil combined. And that mighty power lies within you as a believer in Christ. Decide right now that you will never again let the devil get the upper hand. You were born into the world to face the battle you are in, and the victory is already won. So take your stand and never let the devil intimidate you again with his lies. Now look the devil in the eye and say, "Satan, I reverse your decision right now, in Jesus' name!"

Notes

CHAPTER 1
THE DEVIL WANTS YOU AS HIS SLAVE

1. James Strong, *New Strong's Dictionary of Hebrew and Greek Words,* Electronic Ed., Logos Library System (Nashville: Thomas Nelson, 1997, ©1996), s.v. *"kategoros."*

CHAPTER 5
BETTER THAN A CHILI DOG

1. "The Solid Rock" by Edward Mote and William Bradbury. Public domain.

CHAPTER 7
GOING ON WHEN YOU CAN'T GO ON

1. W. E. Vine, Merrill F. Unger and William White, *Vine's Complete Expository Dictionary of Old and New Testament Words,* Electronic Ed., Logos Library System (Nashville: Thomas Nelson, 1997, ©1996).

2. Gerhard Kittel, and Gerhard Friedrich, editors, *The Theological Dictionary of the New Testament, Abridged in One Volume* (Grand Rapids, MI: William B. Eerdmans Publishing Company, 1985), s.v. *"meno."*

3. John Claypool, *Leadership Journal,* Vol. 12, no. 2, n.p. Other sources: Michael P. Green, *Illustrations for Biblical Preaching* (Grand Rapids, MI: Baker Book House, 1989), s.v. "perseverance"; James S. Hewett, *Illustrations Unlimited* (Wheaton: Tyndale House Publishers, Inc. 1988), 155.

CHAPTER 12
DELIVERANCE FROM DISCOURAGEMENT AND HOPELESSNESS

1. Michael P. Green, *Illustrations for Biblical Preaching* (Grand Rapids, MI: Baker Book House, 1989).

CHAPTER 14
YOU WERE CREATED FOR A PURPOSE

1. *The American Heritage Dictionary of the English Language,* Third Edition, s.v. "purpose."

2. Ibid., s.v. "vague."

Other Ministry Materials by Mike Purkey

MUSIC CDS AND CASSETTE TAPES

I Plead the Blood
A Collection of Favorites
That's What He Is
Revive Us
Hallelujah Anyhow
The Good News Is the Bad News Was Wrong
Let's Have Church

PREACHING AND MUSIC VIDEOS

Having a Time—Mike Purkey and Jesse Duplantis

More Good Times—Mike Purkey and Jesse Duplantis

A Shout in the House—Mike Purkey and Bishop T. D. Jakes

Seasons—Mike Purkey and Bishop T. D. Jakes

My, My, My, What Singin'—Mike Purkey and Karen Wheaton

Mike Purkey and Friends

*Camp Meeting in America's Heartland—Mike Purkey,
Bishop T. D. Jakes, Rod Parsley and Nancy Harmon*

For a free product catalog from Mike Purkey Ministries or
for information on having Mike Purkey minister
at your church, conference or retreat, please contact
the ministry at the following address:

MIKE PURKEY MINISTRIES

P. O. Box 14611
Lenexa, KS 66285-4611
(800) 731-4744
E-mail: visitation@mikepurkey.org

To find out when Mike Purkey will be speaking in
your area or to place online orders for his ministry
materials, visit his website at:
www.mikepurkey.org

Your Walk With God Can Be Even Deeper...

With *Charisma* magazine, you'll be informed and inspired by the features and stories about what the Holy Spirit is doing in the lives of believers today.

Each issue:

- Brings you exclusive world-wide reports to rejoice over.
- Keeps you informed on the latest news from a Christian perspective.
- Includes miracle-filled testimonies to build your faith.
- Gives you access to relevant teaching and exhortation from the most respected Christian leaders of our day.

Call 1-800-829-3346 for 3 FREE trial issues

Offer #AOACHB

If you like what you see, then pay the invoice of $22.97 (**saving over 51% off the cover price**) and receive 9 more issues (12 in all). Otherwise, write "cancel" on the invoice, return it, and owe nothing.

Experience the Power of Spirit-Led Living

Charisma Offer #AOACHB
P.O. Box 420234
Palm Coast, Florida 32142-0234
www.charismamag.com